Escaping The Great Deception

"How shall we escape
if we ignore
such a great salvation?"
HEBREWS 2:3

Derek Frank
with Françoise Frank

Escaping The Great Deception

Published by Roaring Lion Productions, Inc.

Author photos by David Molnar
Cover design by Erik Hollander

ISBN 978-0-9960759-0-9

The lion has roared –

who will not fear?

The Sovereign Lord has spoken –

who can but prophesy?

AMOS 3:8

DEDICATION

This book is dedicated to the Jewish people, through whom we have received so much, and to whom so little has been given back.

Our prayer is that it will hasten the day when “ten men from all languages and nations will take firm hold of one Jew by the hem of his robe and say ‘Let us go with you, because we have heard that God is with you’” (Zechariah 8: 23).

FOREWORD BY DANI JOHNSON

There I was, reading the manuscript of this book on a plane with tears streaming down my face, saying out loud, "Finally, someone is telling the truth! Imagine you and I had been steered in a direction that had robbed us of a great blessing. Is that possible? You bet it is. We then unintentionally build our lives on a half-truth, thinking that it is, in fact, the truth. We even raise our children to believe these half-truths and to live according to them. This equation can rob not only you and your next generation of great blessings, but it can also be very dangerous!

I am sure you have noticed the corruption that exists in the church today. Man exalting himself and being driven by selfish ambition or greed. We have more churches than ever, yet we also have more corruption than ever. Of the hundreds of thousands of people whom I have encountered face-to-face in my life, I have seen with my own eyes multitudes of people disheartened, disillusioned, and downright infuriated by the lack of pure leadership in our churches today. Instead, we have manipulative and self-serving agendas. So, the believers have no passion for truth because they don't know truth. We have become docile, boring, and lifeless! Oh, don't get me wrong, there are some pockets where "things" are happening. However, overall, the majority of the body of Christ is powerless! We have lost our influence in the world, and the so-called believers either haven't realized it or simply don't care.

For more than a decade, I have been exposing the corruption of our current condition to millions of people from all over the world. I have often felt alone in this journey, so when I began to read this book I was stirred again with great passion for this message. I was not crazy; God had revealed the same truths to a precious pastor. And this pastor had the guts to tell the truth to the few who would listen instead of tickling the ears of more people, even though we all know that ear tickling results in big offerings. Pastor Derek Frank has my deep respect for exposing the great deception that has robbed us all for hundreds of years.

This is why I knew that the book in front of me was so important for the whole body of Christ. So much of what we follow today has come from leaders who have been hurt, discouraged, and disillusioned. A theology has been birthed from within unhealed hearts. And we've been blindly following this deception because it is what our fathers and mothers followed. In my case, it was what the church taught - or rather what it did not teach - that almost caused me to walk away from it forever.

When I finally rededicated my life to Christ, I quickly found a huge divide between the Bible and the modern church. As I began to study, I found truths that were simply not spoken of at church. The Bible is filled with accounts of holidays and festivities celebrating all that God has done for His people, and yet we Christians don't celebrate any of them. Instead, we celebrate pagan holidays that glorify fertility gods! When I read the Bible from cover to cover, I saw that from beginning to end it is the love story between God and His chosen people, the Jews. I felt God place such a love for His chosen people into my heart that I knew anything He was so passionate about I was called to be passionate about, too. Yet what I would hear from the pulpit told me nothing about the Jews. It was as though when Jesus died on the cross, the Jews somehow became obsolete, that they were no longer God's chosen people. I felt as though we Christians had been robbed of a rich heritage, of a blessing that could bring us ever so much closer to God, and of a faith that was immovable.

The Bible is filled with stories of God's chosen people and what happens to those who bless them and to those who curse them. Each time I encountered a Jew, I was awestruck, and I would often say to them, "I know we are blessed because you are here." They would look at me strangely and ask why I felt that way. My response was always the same: "You are of the seed of Abraham, and the blood of my Savior runs through your veins."

The more I studied, the more I came to love the Jewish people and to feel drawn to them, to their culture, to their traditions, and to their history. I've learned so much from Abraham, Isaac,

Jacob, Moses, Joseph, Daniel, King David, his son King Solomon, and - obviously - Jesus and His disciples. All these figures have taught me about business, finance, relationships, family, and leadership. They taught me how to fully love and devote myself to God. Then I realized that God chose the Jews - He chose the people of Israel - as the bloodline that would one day birth the Savior. Of all the people in the world, God strategically chose the Jews to bring His own flesh and blood to this earth so that all the rest of the world would be saved from the payment of sin. He chose Israel, not any other nation, to bring the Savior into the world! Do you get that? Do you understand what I am saying?

As God revealed this to me, I was overwhelmed with gratitude for the Jews. The Bible also came alive in a new way. I wanted so badly to know the customs, traditions, tastes, smells, and the way of life of God's chosen people. It somehow gave me a closer sense of how Jesus - a Jew with a Jewish name, Yeshua - may have lived. The holidays He celebrated, the foods He ate. Did He wear a prayer shawl with tassels like the Jews of today? My life became enriched as God lovingly drew me into this understanding. The more I learn, the closer I am pulled to Him.

For some odd reason, I've had a menorah in my house for twenty years now. I've kept the Sabbath since 1996. And since 2005, I've blown the shofar at home and in every city I've traveled to around the world (even in Istanbul, Turkey!) I've also prayed under a tallit (a Jewish prayer shawl) since 2007. The more I became connected to the Jewish people, the closer I felt to the Father, the Son -Yeshua - and the Holy Spirit.

After having four different Jews come to me within a nine-month period and ask me if I were a Jew, I was compelled to do what they had all suggested - to take a DNA test. Each one of those precious people, one of whom was an orthodox Jew, asked me exactly the same questions, and each one stated that his or her Rabbi had read my books and approved of their attendance at my seminars. Each one told me that I taught like their Rabbi and that I knew my Father like a Jew knows his or her Father, as opposed to the way the Christians do. Then finally the truth was uncovered. The DNA test came back, revealing that I was, in fact, a Jew! Everything made perfect sense to me after that test. I had already been teaching children, clients, friends, and the fans of our radio and television shows what I was learning about the Jews, but now it was more than that.... Now I was responsible for making sure that my Gentile brothers and sisters in Messiah (Christ) were no longer robbed of the rich heritage of our Jewish Messiah, Yeshua. I was responsible for making sure they understood the importance and necessity of blessing Israel - that always results in us being blessed, too. I was responsible for making sure they understood that they were grafted into the line of Abraham, Isaac, and Israel through Yeshua, rather than believing the lie that Israel was grafted into them.

When I read the manuscript for this book, I was flabbergasted by the truth that was being so boldly proclaimed across its pages. This book is clearly a message for our generation from the God of Israel. He is exposing something that has been hidden for hundreds of years. I feel so blessed that He has chosen you to hear it. I pray that the Holy Spirit will help you grasp the wisdom contained in the pages of this book. We have been robbed, my friend, by a great deception. Our children have been robbed, and our future generations will continue to be robbed if we remain on the path we are on. We must rally around this message so that we may help our brothers and sisters come into the full understanding of what God has intended for all of us in this generation.

As you read this powerful book, ask the Holy Spirit to guide you through these pages, and get ready for your world to be rocked!!!

– Dani Johnson

CONTENTS

CHAPTER 1

Receiving the Vision

THE VISION WAS BRIEF, yet it was to change my life forever. Each time, I saw the same pictures and heard the same words. Gradually, the words "complete the reformation" became etched on my mind.

I knew it was a prophecy, but it was beyond me to interpret it, let alone work out how to apply it. As the message did not go away, my discomfort got worse. At first, I presumed it was just about finishing something the sixteenth century Reformers had started. So it took a long time before I realized that I was wrong.

In my vision, I would see the outside of an impressive building with an imposing Greek-style entrance, with pillars and steps and a cobblestoned courtyard. People were going in and coming out, dressed in medieval clothing. Then the scene would switch to the inside of the building where many people wearing headsets were attending a twenty-first century conference. The vision always ended with the command to "complete the reformation."

I saw the vision many times. It was twenty-five years ago, during the charismatic wave of the late eighties when I was on the staff of a large church in England. Such visions were more usual then, but no one could interpret mine. Frustrated, I asked God either to explain it or to stop it - and it stopped. I was both relieved and intrigued, but I still wrestled with the same question. How was I to complete the reformation?

Years later, as I made my first visit to the old city of Geneva, Switzerland, the Lord caught me unawares. I already knew that John Calvin, the great Reformer, had preached the Reformation from there. I also had some idea of how he had transformed the city in one generation from being "the stinkiest city in all Europe" to "the most perfect school of Christ that ever was on earth since the days of the apostles."[1] But I was not prepared for what was about to happen when I came around a corner.

I stopped dead. In front of me, precise to the last detail, was the very building I had seen so often in my vision: the Cathedral of St. Pierre, the seat of Calvin's Reformation. For a few minutes, I just stood motionless, shaken to the core and shocked by the enormity of what it might mean. Then my fears gave place to a growing inner conviction that I was called to fulfill a specific mission. It seemed arrogant that I could ever add anything to the Reformers' achievements, yet it became increasingly obvious that some crucial clue was missing. Whatever it was, I instantly knew that I was the one to look for it.

So I went on a treasure hunt and applied myself to explore the depth and length of the Reformation. The scale of this phenomenal achievement was truly beyond me, although it was clear that the newly recovered gospel had been both salvation to the body and salvation to the soul for the masses.

This was the start of a journey of discovery that was to take me on the adventure of a lifetime, a voyage in which I was to uncover a dark and demonic conspiracy that had been perpetuated by church leaders for hundreds of years. It led me to discover one of the greatest and darkest deceptions of our time — the conspiracy to cover up the Church's true identity[2]. It was a journey that was to change my life forever.

Times were grim in medieval Europe. People were sick and tired of lives bound by a fear of evil spirits and eternal damnation. To this, the Church added further burdens through a system of penance for the cleansing of sins, apart from which there could be no absolution. After confession the priest would tell sinners what to do to make amends. Once their penance was completed they were forgiven, but their slate was only wiped clean until the next time. There was still no answer to the question of how death, let alone the Almighty Judge, was to be faced. So the Church came up with the idea of the intermediate state of purgatory. There the dead would supposedly undergo purification to attain holiness, even though the prospect of its cleansing fire was terrifying to Churchgoers. To reduce the agony of the dead the priests sold prayers and masses, but they did so at a price that few could afford. It was highly lucrative for the Church, yet for people whose lives were often short, harsh, and plague ridden, it heightened the ongoing sense of suffering further still.

It drove them to cry out, "How ever can we be right with God? Surely there's a better way to live, a better way to care for our families and to care for the poor?"

Luther's Breakthrough

I learned that this depth of oppression both incensed a young German monk called Martin Luther and exacerbated his acute sense of unworthiness. How could he, a sinner, hold the body and the blood of Christ in his own hands and not incur the wrath of the living God? To atone, he would spend hours confessing his sins, always gripped by the fear that he might have forgotten to mention some. What troubled him most was the intrinsic sin in man, the incontestable evidence that human beings were basically corrupt. Struggling for an answer, he finally came to the conclusion that the answer would have to come directly from God.

Luther was rapidly appointed professor of theology at the University of Wittenberg. There he began to apply the newly found study principle of probing the original texts of scripture to find their true meaning. In 1513, when he was preparing a lecture on the Psalms, he was captivated by the words from Psalm 31:1, "Deliver me in your righteousness."

Luther had always understood righteousness to be God's punishment of sinful man, but this time he saw it differently. So he carried on searching and came across Romans 1:17, "A righteousness, that is by faith from first to last."

Now that we understand what this scripture means, it is hard for us to appreciate Luther's tremendous inner battle. Single-handedly, he broke the stronghold that righteousness could only be achieved by works, a lie that had kept the Church in bondage for a thousand years. He uncovered the truth that man is made right with God by faith alone. He saw that righteousness could not be beaten into man by a process of punishments but had to be received as a gift from a merciful and forgiving God.

This was Luther's breakthrough to freedom. His years of anguish were over, and now with great joy he was able to say, "I felt myself to be reborn and to have gone through open doors into paradise. The whole scripture took on a new meaning, and whereas before the 'righteousness of God' had filled me with hate, now it became to me inexpressibly sweet in greater love. This passage in Paul became to me a gateway to heaven."[3]

But it was not long before his joy turned to anger as the corruption of the Catholic Church became even more intolerable. The scandalous sale of indulgences, which claimed to release souls from purgatory, was the last straw. So to challenge the

Church and open a debate, he nailed his ninety-five theses on the door of the Castle Church in Wittenburg. He was not planning anything like a Reformation; he was simply wanting to see truth restored to the established Church. But the news spread like wildfire, and the surge of interest spurred him to write more and more, causing his message to go viral. With the help of the newly invented printing press, it had an explosive impact. The people just could not get enough of it.

Many were converted, among them a young lawyer in Paris called Jean Calvin. Following Luther's footsteps, Calvin published his *Institutes of the Christian Religion*, which soon became very popular. Through them, he wanted believers to return to the original beliefs and practice of the Church.

Calvin's Agenda

In 1536, by a God-incidence, Calvin's travels were diverted through Geneva, Switzerland. The citizens had just evicted the Catholic authorities. Now leaderless, they were contending with a reform-shaped vacuum but were determined to "live henceforth according to the Law of the gospel and the Word of God and to abolish all papal abuses."[4]

As they had heard of Calvin's famous writings, they begged him to stay to govern the city. Because of their immoral lifestyle, he only agreed reluctantly, and a bumpy ride followed for both parties. Later on, Calvin would speak of Geneva as "that cross on which I had to perish daily a thousand times over."[5]

By enforcing strict adherence to biblical precepts, he managed to suppress corruption within the walled city and impose his vision of a "visible city of God." Geneva rapidly became a working model of the gospel's relevance to every area of life. It was based entirely on rightness with God without a priest as an intermediary. It was completely by grace and totally through faith. Answers were first to be found in the Bible rather than in the Church, because unlike the Church, it gave values for the whole of life. Those values brought forth individual responsibility, education for all, care of the poor, accountability in government, and much more. So much so that this pilot "city state" became a blueprint for a successful nation built on biblical principles.

For those who had known the Geneva of old, its transformation was striking. Because of its situation at the crossroads of trade routes that ran both north-south and east-west, its influence quickly spread outward. It also attracted Reformation-minded thinkers and protestant refugees from other countries, who brought with them the skills that were to make the city prosperous.

The Missing Clue

The Reformation was an astounding achievement. However, even though many gaps were later filled, much was left incomplete in the Reformers' lifetime. But this still did not give me any clue as to what I was supposed to find. If anything, it only raised more questions and left me wondering whatever "complete the reformation" meant.

Then one day, I unexpectedly stumbled across a story that was to connect many dots.

When Protestantism was declared illegal in nearby France, individuals and cities faced the choice of declaring their allegiance to the Catholic Church or martyrdom. Geneva welcomed them in and soon became known as the City of Refuge for persecuted Protestants. As a result, it quickly doubled its population from ten to twenty thousand.

So I was shocked to find that the Jews were banned from living in Geneva.

Anti-Semitism had been rife across Europe long before the Reformation, and it had been prevalent throughout the Middle Ages from the fifth century onward. It was a hate movement loosely based on holding the Jews responsible for the murder of Jesus, fuelled by the religious rhetoric of the Crusaders of the 1096 Crusade. They had declared that the Jews who were part of the local community were as much of an enemy as the distant Muslims who ruled Jerusalem. It was one of the many reasons which had led to the anti-Jewish legislation of Pope Innocent III. In 1215, he had decreed that all Jews should wear an identity mark on their clothes so that no one could possibly confuse them with Christians.

As the Pope was bent on preventing Christians from associating with Jews, they were increasingly segregated into crowded ghettos. They were treated as the outcasts of medieval Europe and identified as a people who deserved to be cursed. They became a scapegoat for everyone's woes, and as a result, hundreds of thousands of them died.

Not surprisingly, Geneva, with its dubious moral climate, was no exception to the rule. When the Black Death of 1350 struck, the Jews were accused of poisoning the wells, and many were put to death. Finally, in 1490, they were completely driven out and forced to pay a daily toll to enter the city.

It was three hundred years before they were allowed to live in the city again.[6] Most significantly, it meant that although they were expulsed fifty years before Calvin's arrival, their expulsion was only reversed two hundred years after his death.

This did not fit in with the image of a city that lived according to biblical principles. It gave me a hunch that I was getting closer to whatever I was to uncover. I now knew that however much else Calvin had successfully addressed, he had not addressed the issue of anti-Semitism.

Subliminal or not, his message appeared to be "Whatever else the newly recovered gospel is changing, one thing which is not for changing is the view we've always had of the Jewish people."

Some Searching Questions

Should he have allowed the Jews to take refuge in his "model city of God," Calvin would have had to confront anti-Semitism head on. So why had he not done it? Had he lacked the nerve? Was it just not his priority over all that was clamoring for his attention? Or, most disturbingly, was it actually his deliberate choice to do nothing?

Determined to get to the bottom of it, I decided to investigate where Luther had stood on the subject.

I soon found out that where he ended up on anti-Semitism was not where he had begun. Initially, Luther had tried very hard to tackle it. Incensed by the Church's demonization of the Jews, he had vehemently denounced it, saying, "They have dealt with the Jews as though they were dogs and not human beings. They have done nothing for them but curse them and seize their wealth. I would advise and beg everybody to deal kindly with the Jews and instruct them in the scriptures. In such a case, we could expect them to come over to us . . . we must receive them kindly and allow them to compete with us in earning a livelihood . . . and if some remain obstinate, what of it?"[7]

For this, the Vatican had called him a "half Jew." Taking the moral high ground, Luther mocked them, saying, "They, the Jews, are blood brothers of our Lord. If it were proper to boast of flesh and blood, the Jews belong to Christ more than we. I beg, therefore, my dear Papists, if you become tired of abusing me as a heretic, that you begin to revile me as a Jew."[8]

Luther fully expected the Jews to convert; however, they were comfortable in their Judaism and did not budge. Cruelly disappointed and then extremely outraged, Luther suddenly turned against them. As passionately as he had blessed them before, he now cursed them with a sixty-five thousand word treatise he entitled *On the Jews and Their Lies,* saying, "Burn their synagogues and schools; what will not burn, bury it with earth that neither stone nor rubbish remain. In like manner break into and destroy their homes. Take away their prayer book and Talmuds. For in them there is nothing but godlessness, lies, cursing, and swearing. Forbid their Rabbis to teach, on pain of life or limb."[9]

Some attributed Luther's bitterness to failing health, and others to his frustration with the German peasants who were misusing the banner of Protestantism to fight serfdom. Nevertheless, when I studied this text, these words jumped off the page at me "In such case . . . we could expect them to come over to us."

This statement clearly exposed Luther's view of the Jewish people. It showed how for him the Church was no more than a Gentile bubble. He obviously thought that the Jews had to become culturally Gentile in order to receive salvation. He was effectively declaring that the Church had replaced Israel as the focus of God's choice in the outworking of His purposes. Although he believed that the Jewish people had been God's chosen nation in the past, he believed they no longer were. He had then concluded that if they had lost favor with God, they only had themselves to blame.

This drove me to dig deeper. I had to find out what Calvin's position was.

Calvin's View

When Luther died in 1546, Geneva was coming into its own as the great city of the Reformation. Although he had not sought it, Calvin had an opportunity which Luther had never had. Regardless of his unorthodox methods, he was the supreme governor of Geneva. He could road test the principles of the Reformation on a city which was generally compliant, if only because of his tribunals. His position gave him the authority to establish and maintain a "visible city of God," which in turn increased the ripple effect of the Reformation.

The fact that Calvin had not allowed the Jewish people to return to Geneva was therefore immensely significant. He had sent a clear signal that whatever the Reformation had changed it would not change the reputation of the Jewish people. The question was why? Was it an oversight? Was it a lack of motivation because of Luther's previous experience with them? Or was it that a Geneva already free of Jews was most convenient to him, lest they debased his "model city of God"?

As I continued searching, I found that Calvin, a brilliant scholar, had an extensive knowledge of the Old Testament. Having avidly studied the Hebraic texts, he had been sympathetic to the historical significance of Israel, but that is where his sympathy had stopped. This indicated that his ignoring the problem of anti-Semitism was neither an oversight nor a lack of interest but a very deliberate choice.

In fact, some of his quotes revealed that he viewed the Jews' current significance differently from what it had been in the past.

When he had been more polite, he had written, "I have had much conversation with many Jews: I have never seen either a drop of piety or a grain of truth or ingenuousness — nay, I have never found common sense in any Jew."[10] When less polite, he had written that the Jews' "rotten and unbending stiff-neckedness deserves that they be oppressed unendingly and without measure or end and that they die in their misery without the pity of anyone."[11] And when commenting on Romans 11:26 about "and so all Israel shall be saved," he had dogmatically asserted that "the Israel of God is what Paul calls the Church."[12]

Quoting Galatians 6:16, which speaks of the Israel of God, he had consolidated his position and said, "There are two classes who bear this name, a pretended Israel which appears to be so in the sight of men — and the Israel of God."[13] So I was left in no doubt that Calvin was on the same page as Luther regarding the Jews who had not "come over to us."

For him, the idea that the Jews were still God's chosen nation was no more than a pretense. By this, he had implied that God had transferred all the covenants and promises to the Church, which had become the "new and improved" version of Israel.[14]

In Luther's latter words, it meant that since the Jews had rejected Jesus, "the only things left to them were the curses found in the Bible, but none of the blessings."[15]

This message that the Church had replaced Israel was then intricately woven into the fabric of the newly recovered gospel. Because people's lives were radically improved by the Reformation, and it was commonly accepted that the Jews were supposedly accursed, no one had had any reason to dispute it. And as this message was passed from one generation of the Church to the next, it became increasingly established as the truth.

However, I knew that Calvin and Luther's positions were not an absolute guarantee of truth. They might still have both been insidiously deceived. And if they had, it would have put a serious fault line through the gospel that was handed down to us.

So was this the great incompletion of the Reformation I was looking for?

CHAPTER 2

Putting It to the Test

TO SPECULATE THAT THE Reformers were not just mistaken, but perhaps even deceived, was audacious. To put them on trial seemed disrespectful and presumptuous in the extreme.

There was much for which I was grateful to Luther and Calvin, and I had a list of reasons to prove it. I was in awe of their endurance to fight for truth until they got their breakthrough. I was also humbled by their outstanding leadership. With great courage, they had confronted the established Church and reformed its corrupt theology. In their pragmatism, they had implemented the recovered gospel into the ordinary man's every day. Their prodigious grasp of scripture and their own writings had left an impressive legacy. Most inspiringly, they had given their all for it.

I certainly did not want to be like the Counter-reformers, who had sought to desecrate both the memories and the groundbreaking work of the Reformers.

Yet Calvin's very intentional position regarding the ongoing significance of the Jews bothered me deeply, and I was compelled to put this to the test.

From the very start, the purpose of Calvin's teaching had been to regenerate the original beliefs of the Church. But this rang alarm bells for me. Had Calvin taken his position on the basis of theological statements found in earlier Christianity? If so, had its leaders been mistaken and deceived as well?

Given the rise of anti-Semitism from the fourth century onward, I wondered if Constantine's conversion in AD 313 had been a pivotal point for it. This had led to huge numbers of Gentile conversions, which had turned what was originally a Jewish community into a predominantly Gentile one. This seemed to be as good a place as any to investigate.

It did not take me long to find out how the Reformers' anti-Semitic teaching had actually sprung out of declarations made by many Church fathers a thousand years beforehand. I was horrified by a series of hate-filled statements.

Hilary, Bishop of Poitiers (AD 300–368), who refused to eat with the Jews, wrote, "The Jews are a people who glorified iniquity."[1]

Jerome (AD 325–420) professed, "There could never be expiation for the Jews: God has always hated them."[2]

Bishop John Chrysostom (AD 347–407) published a series of sermons that expressed intense hatred and malice toward the Jews, stating, “Because God hates the Jews, it is the duty of Christians to hate them.” “Many, I know, respect the Jews and think their present way of life is a venerable one. This is why I hasten to uproot and tear down this terrible opinion . . . the synagogue is not only a brothel and a theatre, it is also a den of robbers and a lodging for wild beasts . . . when God forsakes a people, what hope of salvation is left? When God forsakes a place, that place becomes the dwelling of demons.”[3]

Ambrose, Bishop of Milan (AD 340–397), said, “I declare that I have set fire to the synagogue, or at least that those who did it acted under my orders, so that there would be no place where Christ is rejected . . . Moreover, the synagogue was in fact destroyed by the judgment of God.”[4]

Augustine of Hippo (AD 354-430), known as one of the greatest Christian thinkers of all time, berated the Jews mercilessly with pernicious statements such as “The Jews were sons of God, but now they are the sons of Satan. The true image of the Hebrews is Judas Iscariot, who sells the Lord for silver. The Jew can never understand the scriptures and will forever bear the guilt of Jesus.”[5]

To these statements could be added those of Eusebius, Hippolytus, and of many other prominent names in the early Church.

To make matters worse, Jews who came to faith in Jesus were ordered to break all ties with their own people and their Jewish traditions. They were forced to publicly confess "I renounce all customs, rites, legalisms, unleavened breads and sacrifices of lambs of the Hebrews, and all other feasts of the Hebrews, sacrifices, prayers, purifications, Sabbaths . . . In one word I renounce absolutely everything Jewish, every law, rite and custom . . . and if I wish to deny and return to Jewish superstition . . . then let the trembling of Cain and the leprosy of Gehazi cleave to me . . . And may I be anathema in the world to come, and may my soul be set down with Satan and the devils."[6]

It was clear that Luther and Calvin had followed a trend that dated back to the fourth century at least. This trend had implied that God was "finished with the Jews" and had no ongoing purpose for the nation of Israel. It had even gone as far as replacing meaningful biblical Hebrew names with Gentile ones. We can only speculate about the extent of the demonic strategy that lay behind the stripping of these names. Especially because there is power in honoring the name of Yeshua, Jesus' real name, which means "God is salvation".

However, regardless of their prominence and apparent respectability, these venerated Church leaders were by no means infallible or beyond being deceived.

Tough Questions

In the midst of this, God reminded me of the words that He had spoken to Israel around two thousand five hundred years ago. "I have loved you with an everlasting love."[7] "'Only if the heavens above can be measured and the foundations of the earth below be searched out will I reject all the descendants of Israel because of all they have done' declares the Lord."[8] "O Israel: 'Fear not, for I have redeemed you: I have summoned you by name; you are mine.'"[9]

He reminded me that even earlier He had promised Israel,

"If you obey me fully and keep my covenant, then out of all nations, you will be my treasured possession."[10] And that earlier still He had given this eternal promise to Abram, "I will establish my covenant as an everlasting covenant between me and you and your descendants after you . . ."[11]

He also reminded me of Paul's penetrating argument, which confirmed Israel's ongoing purpose in the New Covenant, "Did God reject His people? By no means!"[12] "As far as election is concerned, they are loved on account of the patriarchs, for God's gifts and his call are irrevocable."[13]

Now I was bemused. Given that God means what He says, it would be a surprising U-turn if He had changed His mind and reneged on the Jews because of their disobedience. So why did the Reformers' interpretation of these texts redefine the irrevocability of God's promises to them? This was most disturbing.

Would God change His mind about the body of believers too because of its sin and compromise? Could this affect our own salvation? What about Israel? Would its ongoing significance now depend on its acceptance of Yeshua as its Messiah?

I wished I could meet Calvin to dialogue with him face to face. So I imagined him squeezing me into his frenetic schedule. But I figured I might only get as far as saying "the Jews . . ." before he would cut me short with "No one comes to the Father except by me!"[14]

Then he might say "How can the Jewish people who do not accept Jesus have any standing with God?"

And he might also want to drum into me that "It is by grace that you have been saved, through faith."[15] "There is no exception clause, even for the Jewish people from whom our Lord came." At this point I would just have to thank him and leave.

For the Reformers, personal salvation was fundamental to everything else. The touchstone of the Reformation was "from first to last that righteousness was by faith." Without it there was no right standing with God. This was so important to them that the plight of the Jews and the significance of Israel were by comparison quite irrelevant.

However, I imagined meeting Calvin again, this time to discuss today's nation-state of Israel.

Having scarcely started, he might soon interrupt me with "Are you telling me that these people are there in repentance and that their nation's values honor God's name?" He might make the point that they did not look anything like the chosen people of God, but would still struggle to explain their return to the land as an accident of history.

There were truly many tough questions, and I was desperate for wisdom. I needed solid answers, especially if the Jews were the clue to completing the Reformation. To my relief, guidance came through the words of 1 Timothy 5:19, "Do not entertain an accusation against an elder unless it is brought by two or three witnesses."[16]

I was grateful when I realized that I had three witnesses: the city of Geneva, the Jewish people, and the Protestant Church.

IN THE COURTROOM

So in the courtroom of my imagination, I called my first witness, the city of Geneva.

To the city of Geneva, I asked, "How did things go on for you following the Reformation?"

Geneva answered, "For the next generation or two, things carried on much as they had under Calvin. When he died in 1564, Theodore Beza took over. Although under his leadership we still maintained Calvin's disciplines, it was more relaxed as he was less severe. We continued to flourish, at least in a material way, as we do four hundred and fifty years on. Here today, you can find the United Nations and the headquarters of many international organizations like the World Trade Organization, the World Health Organization, and even the World Council of Churches. A fair slice of the world's private finance passes through our banks. Much is brokered in Geneva, often secretly and with worldwide impact. Despite being small in global terms, we have affluence and influence out of all proportion to our size."

Curious, I asked, "How has it been for the community of believers in Geneva?"

Geneva replied, "Spiritually, there has been much apathy. In fact, apart from a revival in the early 1800s, that's how it has been for centuries. Even when Voltaire arrived here in the 1700s, he said, 'I looked for a pastor who believed in God, but couldn't find one.' What really undermined it though was the Enlightenment. It was like a flooding river washing away a building's foundations. It started in the late 1600s when it began to promote rationalism. Rational logic then brought such progress that it gained great credibility and anything that it couldn't prove was devalued, especially faith. This left our church in a catch up mode. It tried to make the gospel look relevant by reducing it to only what rational logic would accept. The hearts of the pastors went cold. Jesus was downgraded to being nothing more than an enlightened moral teacher. Skepticism and criticism replaced faith, and just about everything Calvin had accomplished here spiritually was undone within one hundred and fifty years."

Grieved, I then asked, "Does God's admonition to the Ephesian church 'you have forsaken your first love' apply to you too?"

Geneva replied, "Very sadly, yes. Our lamp stand was removed from us, and apart from a few brief spells, it has not been replaced."

I heard myself say, "Thank you, city of Geneva, you may stand down. Call the second witness."

To the Jewish people, I then asked, "How did things go on for you following the Reformation?"

The Jewish people angrily replied, "For us, the Reformation changed nothing. The cruel persecution we'd known beforehand carried on afterward. You know what it led to. Let us just say a few names, like Kristallnacht . . . Auschwitz . . . Dachau . . . Ravensbruck. How could such things have been done to us, just because we were Jews? How could Hitler claim that in persecuting us, he was simply doing what the Church had done for sixteen hundred years?[17] We could say so much more. But do we really need to?"

Humbled, I whispered, "I don't think you do. We deeply respect your testimony Jewish people. Please call the third witness."

To the Protestant Church, I asked, "How did things go on for you following the Reformation?"

The Protestant Church replied despondently, "It was the Reformation that birthed us. It gave us our gospel and reached out to millions, but sadly we were divided from the beginning. Our founders, the Reformers, disagreed from the start. Today we are fragmented into thousands of different denominations and are only a tiny minority. We can hardly claim to be the salt and light of the world."

I continued, "What about the genuine faith which is still there in the Church?"

The Protestant Church replied, "Even when there is real faith, it is generally personal and private. Rather like a sweater that's taken on and off, so is much of the faith expressed on Sundays. It has been said that 'the Church is sleeping whilst God is weeping.' This may well explain why in the west we hardly face any persecution. As you know, a sleeping tiger is far less dangerous than a wounded one. Many of us are into religion rather than relationship with God. We tolerate all sorts of unrighteousness. We strain gnats but swallow camels. We should be roaring like a lion, but the fact is that we're only whimpering . . ."

I thanked the Protestant Church for its honesty. The trial was over.

The Verdict

The facts were undeniable. Despite its amazing achievements, these three tragic testimonies demonstrated that the Reformation was seriously flawed and blatantly incomplete.

I left the courtroom heavy-hearted. I wondered how different a verdict it would have been if the Reformers had stressed Paul's picture of the olive tree in Romans 11, which describes believers being "grafted in" to Israel. What if instead of presuming as Luther had done, it was all about "them coming over to us" they had understood it was all about "us going over to them"?

This would have positively endorsed God's ongoing purpose for Israel. It would have also dramatically changed the tragic impact that anti-Semitism had on Geneva, on the Jewish people, and on the Church.

For Geneva, Calvin's motto "Post Tenebras Lux" (meaning "after the darkness light") soon rang hollow. Sadly, God's opportunity to once again use this city as a model to the world was lost. With it, Geneva might have provided boundaries for the rationalism of the Enlightenment rather than letting it ride roughshod over everything it stood for. One hundred and fifty years of submission to God's plan for the Jews would have been a good training to live out how "my thoughts are not your thoughts, neither are your ways my ways."[18]

And as Paul put it, "O the depth of the riches of the wisdom and knowledge of God! How unsearchable his judgments, and his paths beyond tracing out! Who has known the mind of the Lord? Or who has been his counselor? Who has ever given to God, that God should repay him?"[19]

Had the believers in Geneva humbly recognized God's choice of the Jewish people, it might have withstood the Enlightenment and experienced another season of His great blessing.

As for the Jews, they might have escaped much of the persecution that followed. They might have been less prejudiced against Christianity and more favorable to the gospel, which was for them "first."[20]

What then about the global Church? Had it understood the significance of the nation of Israel, it might have stood with Israel through its history rather than remain aloof as it has done to this day.

In the courtyard of the St. Pierre Cathedral, from which Calvin often preached, is an inconspicuous statue of the prophet Jeremiah. Intriguingly, his face is turned away from the building as if he cannot bear to look at it. His sober words to the deceived people of God still ring true, "They weary themselves with sinning . . . in their deceit they refuse to acknowledge me."[21]

Prophesying over two baskets of figs, Jeremiah had declared, "The good ones are very good, but the poor ones are so bad that they cannot be eaten."[22]

This is a sad picture of the people of God then, and it is a sad picture of the Church today. It produces some good fruit as well as some very rotten fruit because it has not been nourished with the sap it needs.[23] Even when their roots are good, trees need to be in the right soil to produce nourishing sap. Church history might have been very different if it had been rooted in God's chosen soil.

How seriously mistaken the Reformers were to believe that Israel had finally "lost it with God." They had been caught in a Great Deception, a deception which is still alive and active today. Whatever else they had reformed, they had regenerated this lie rather than reformed it.

This revelation determined my next step. I had to find out how the Great Deception could have gained such traction across almost two thousand years of history.

CHAPTER 3

Penetrating the Great Deception

A DECEPTION THAT COULD ENSNARE both the Reformers and their predecessors would have required the most audacious of lies. Its shameless nature and its cunning distortion of God's Word betrayed the most diabolical of strategies.

The further I dug into the deception, the more outrageous I found the claim that the Jews had forfeited their calling.

The fact was, and still is, that without Israel's Jewish Messiah and without Yeshua's Jewish disciples, there would be no Church today.

By striking at the Jewishness of the Christian faith, Satan was going for the jugular. But his vanity was actually the giveaway.

The gospel of Matthew begins with Yeshua's genealogy going as far back as Abraham. Yeshua was born into a Jewish family and raised in the Jewish tradition. He lived and died as a Jew in the land of Israel. His parents Mary and Joseph, the early disciples and the Holy Scriptures, were all Jewish. And even when He healed the Canaanite woman, Yeshua declared that He was sent "only to the lost sheep of Israel."[1]

Yeshua was totally Jewish through and through. Indeed, none of His teaching would have caused the disciples to question the ongoing relevance of their Jewish faith.

The first disciples continued to celebrate Pentecost and pray at the temple after Yeshua's death. Paul attended the synagogue and kept the law throughout his life.[2] And to consider how far Gentile believers should embrace the Jewish law, the apostles convened a council in Jerusalem.[3] For the elders of the early Messianic community, faith in Yeshua was inseparable from being Jewish.

In many ways, it was a straightforward progression for them because, to quote Alister McGrath, "the Jewish Christians seemed to regard Christianity as an affirmation of every aspect of contemporary Judaism, with the addition of one extra belief - that Jesus was the Messiah."[4]

The manhood of Yeshua was clearly essential in enabling Him to bring salvation from God to men. 1 Timothy 2:5 says, "For there is one God and one mediator between God and men, the man Christ Jesus, who gave himself as a ransom for all men."

God had evidently decided that His manhood should be traditionally Jewish, and so Yeshua was bar mitzvahed in

Jerusalem at Passover,[5] attended the synagogue on Shabbat,[6] and celebrated the three mandatory feasts required by the Torah. He dressed like any other Jewish man of his time, ate like one, and behaved like one. His Jewishness was irrefutably and absolutely intrinsic to His human identity.

He was not the blue-eyed blond Greek god depicted throughout centuries of art and music. He was a Middle Eastern Jewish rabbi who spoke Aramaic and who wore the yarmulke, the tallit and the tzitzit.

Although this thought was not unfamiliar to me, I suspected that Yeshua's Jewishness was much more than just having to belong to some specific ethnic group. I eventually found the clue I was looking for in the words of Revelation 22:16, "I, Jesus, have sent my angel to give you this testimony for the churches. I am the Root and the Offspring of David."

In these last words of scripture, Yeshua was emphatically endorsing the significance of His earthly lineage. His identity as "the Root and Offspring of David" connected Him right back to the promise made to his ancestor Abraham, "Through your offspring all nations of earth will be blessed."[7] Even more importantly, it was to be the final key that would unlock the mystery of the book of Revelation.

The Messianic Line

Yeshua's genealogy identified Him as being of the Messianic line, which stemmed from Abraham. It was to be through Isaac, not Ishmael; through Jacob, not Esau; through Judah, one of the twelve tribes; and then through Jesse with this promise, "A shoot will come up from the stump of Jesse; from his roots a Branch will bear fruit. The Spirit of the Lord will rest upon him . . . With righteousness he will judge the needy, with justice he will give decisions for the poor of the earth. He will strike the earth with the rod of his mouth; with the breath of his lips he will slay the wicked. Righteousness will be his belt and faithfulness the sash round his waist."[8]

Because David was the offspring of Jesse, the title "Son of David" was used by Jews who were looking for the Messiah. When Yeshua called himself the "Son of David," He was publicly announcing that He was the fulfillment of God's promised salvation.

I suddenly realized how pivotal this was in understanding salvation. In fact it was so crucial that it came with a severe warning in Revelation 22:19, "If anybody takes words away from this book of prophecy, God will take away from him his share in the tree of life and in the holy city, which are described in this book."

It was now clear to me that honoring the Messianic line was part and parcel of God's master plan of salvation for all eternity. Because of it, Yeshua's timeless words following Satan's final defeat resounded loud and clear, "I am the Root and the offspring of David."

The proximity of these two verses was manifestly intended. It warned believers that if they were to separate the meaning of one verse from the other, it was at their own peril. God was serious about believers honoring the Messianic line, past, present, and future. Yeshua was, is, and would always be the "root of David" and the "Lion of the tribe of Judah."

In the book of Revelation, when John weeps because no one is worthy to open the scroll, the elder who speaks to him makes this profound connection "Do not weep! See, the Lion of the tribe of Judah, the Root of David, has triumphed."[9]

The heavenly perspective of the Messianic line cannot be downplayed or ignored. No one can tell how much the devil knew of it prior to the coming of the Messiah. But judging by his relentless attempts to destroy Israel from its very inception, it is probable that he had some inkling of it. His aim was to obliterate Israel from the start, both to sabotage the outworking of God's salvation on earth and to avoid being thrown into the lake of fire at the end of time.

His repeated strategy is especially blatant in the book of Esther. It is the story of Haman, an egomaniacal Persian official lusting for the adulation of men. It is also the story of Mordecai, a Jew who would not bow his knee to anyone but the God of Abraham, Isaac, and Jacob. It is furthermore the story of how Esther, a Jewess who became Queen, courageously stepped forward to expose and prevent Haman's evil plot to annihilate her people.

Behind the scenes was the real story, one of a cosmic battle between God and Lucifer, His fallen archangel.

Through Haman, the father of lies manipulated the ignorant King Xerxes into a hatred of the Jewish people. He then tricked him into writing a murderous decree to eradicate the Jews everywhere on a single day by killing them mercilessly.[10]

And following Yeshua's birth, we see a similar attempt at stamping out the Jewish people. A paranoiac king set out to murder all the little boys younger than two years in and around Bethlehem.

By the time Satan tried the same approach directly on Yeshua, he was not so subtle about it. It happened at the highest point of the temple and at the lowest point of Gethsemane. But when he did not succeed in aborting the journey to the cross, he unleashed his hatred on the newly birthed church, the body of Messiah on earth. He planned to sever it from its Messianic lineage so that it would lose its way and wander into compromise.

Centuries later, another psychopath rose to power. He was on a mission to exterminate the Jews to the last, all the way to the gas chambers, so that the world would be "Judenfrei" (Jew free).

And disturbingly today, there is a developing catalogue of events which plainly demonstrate that anti-Semitism is still going strong.

When Muslim rhetoric incites the Arab world to wipe Israel off the map with inflammatory statements, the world often stays silent. When intimidating threats are made that anybody who acknowledges Israel will burn in the fire of Islamic fury, few dare to make a move. When Jews are publicly insulted and humiliated in libelous broadcasts, they remain largely undefended.

Closer home anti-Semitism, "the raw, primitive, street hatred of the Jews,"[11] is on the rise, especially in Europe. Events include Jewish tombstones desecrated with swastikas, defamatory cartoons of stereotyped Jews, vandalizing of Jewish properties and Jews beaten up just for being Jewish.

These events are widely tolerated as legitimate hostility toward Israel, and as it was at the Reformation, the Jews are perceived as having only themselves to blame.

THE DESPERATE PLAN

All this reflects the desperation that lay behind the devil's plan. After the feast of Pentecost, the gospel went beyond the boundaries of Israel, and Gentiles were turning in great numbers toward the very nation that he was plotting to destroy.

Nothing was more urgent than to stop this spiritual awakening from escalating any further. The intervention had to be radical and final. The very memory of Israel had to be erased from the church. There was to be no trace of its ongoing significance, no possible connection between Yeshua and the Root and offspring of David, no link between the Lamb of God and the Lion of the tribe of Judah.

But it was not going to be easy. The newly born body of believers was mostly Jewish, and faith in Yeshua was a natural completion of Judaism. Because there was no immediate way in, Satan waited a couple of centuries for an opportune time.

Meanwhile, he drip fed the ever-growing Gentile fellowship the lie that the Church had replaced Israel. This led to what we now know as replacement theology. Becoming increasingly desensitized and deceived, the Church progressively lost its perspective.

The plan bore his infernal trademarks, and it reflected his ultimate motive. "I will ascend to heaven; I will raise my throne above the stars of God . . . I will ascend above the tops of the clouds, I will make myself like the Most High."[12]

Satan's aim was to kill two birds with one stone. First, it was to snare the Church. Then it was to grievously injure "the apple of God's eye,"[13] the nation that so riled him.

Since the Garden of Eden, he had refined the art of seduction and manipulation, especially when pride and envy were at stake. So he simply whispered to the body of believers, "Did God really say that Israel is still significant?"

The hook was that if salvation was personal and exclusively through Jesus, this was then the whole package. By displacing

Israel, the Church was elevated. It bought the lie that significance belongs to those who apparently deserve it and lost sight of its own true identity and destiny. As it slipped into religiosity, the power of its early days waned. Its grip on the gospel weakened, and its fruit degenerated. The further it drifted away from the truth, the less objective it became about the plight of the Jews. It distanced itself from them and increasingly despised them for rejecting its savior. The way was now wide open for anti-Semitism to be unleashed.

By the time the Reformation came, the deception was so entrenched that it slipped under the radar. As it wove itself into the recovered gospel, it picked up a whole new lease of life. And to this day, it shapes the understanding of many believers who have no perception of how insidious it really is.

So what should we make of the power of replacement theology to mislead our fellow believers? The Bible is clear that just before his final destruction, "Satan will be released from his prison and will go out to deceive the nations in the four corners of the earth."[14] We are warned not to underestimate his power to deceive right up to the end. We saw it when he hit back after the Messianic community was born. We saw it at the Reformation. We have seen it since and we will see it again.

Yeshua warned that in the end times, the devil's strategy will be "to deceive the elect — if that were possible"[15] such that "because of the increase of wickedness, the love of most will grow cold."[16]

To the end, the devil's tactics will remain the same.

First, he will distance individuals from God on the issue of Israel and use wickedness as a wedge to separate them even further from Him.

Second, he will isolate the nation of Israel from the world, leaving it unsupported by a Church which is blind to the truth that the gospel is "first for the Jew and then for the Gentile."[17]

Third, he will focus the witness of the Church on personal salvation, to deter it from impacting the nations and from restoring God's righteousness to the whole earth.

Beyond these pernicious schemes lies Satan's greatest goal, which is to frustrate the master's plan that "through the church, the manifold wisdom of God should be made known to the rulers and authorities in the heavenly realms, according to his eternal purpose which he accomplished in Christ Jesus."[18]

This speaks of the supreme reality that all heaven is watching the unfolding story of God's salvation on earth. It also speaks of how the body of believers is to reflect to the whole created order the tremendous love of the one who created it all. As Ray Stedman wrote, "And as the angels watch us, they see us learn to trust God, to turn from our fears and to renew ourselves with divine strength, to draw upon God's great and mighty promises in the hour of pressure and danger. As they see this, their praise begins to ring out in amazement and wonder at God - who is also able to find a way by which He can lavish His love upon the very ones who deserve His wrath. This makes the angels praise Him."[19]

What a calling, a calling that makes the devil tremble.

DECONSTRUCTING THE ANCIENT LIE

I had traveled a long way in my search since I had first heard the enigmatic words "complete the reformation." The deeper I dug, the clearer I was about what needed to be resolved, but the extent and ramifications of the lie through history seemed to make it untouchable. Whatever the task, it felt impossible.

Then God gave me a vivid picture of a long-established ivy that had grown out of control across a large wall. It had sunk its tendrils into the cracks of the brickwork and spread everywhere. Getting rid of the ivy by picking off one tendril at a time would obviously take forever. The only solution was to take a sharp axe to its roots.

In that moment, I understood that the Great Deception was like this ivy that softened the building's appearance, blending it into the landscape while actually tearing the wall apart. It had given the Church a semblance of sacrosanct respectability, just as ivy gives an ancestral look to a large stately home. Yet under the camouflage, hidden structural damage was taking place.

With the lie, as with the ivy, no amount of picking off every tough question about the significance of Israel could restore the devastating damage of time. The axe had to go to the root of the lie. There was no other way.

However, axing the root of the ivy would still not kill it instantly. It would continue to live until its sap ran out. But once its tendrils lost their grip, it would die and could then be easily pulled off the wall.

In the same way, if the axe went to the root of the deception, the ancient lie would eventually wither and die. Then the truth could be fully declared. To Yeshua's question, "Who do people say the Son of man is?"[20] the Church would be free to boldly reply, "You are the Messiah, the Son of the living God, the Jewish 'Messiah.'"

It is on this foundational statement that Yeshua determined He would build his body on earth. With the two keys of the Kingdom — the full gospel of salvation and its rootedness in Israel — the Messianic community, both Jewish and Gentile, would then become the salt of the earth and the light of the world.

The tyranny of the ivy was calling for action. Now was God's appointed time to sharpen the axe on the grindstone of truth.

CHAPTER 4

Sowing the Seed of Truth

IN THE PARABLE OF the sower, Yeshua was speaking of Himself when He spoke of the Word of God as the seed.[1,2] He was the offspring of Abraham through Isaac and Jacob and the seed deposited into Mary's womb by the power of the Holy Spirit. He was born to die, to be buried, and to rise again to life, to restore the Kingdom first to the Jews and then through them to all the nations.

It was God's prerogative to bring salvation to mankind in a Jewish way. This is still His choice to this day. We might want to argue it with the God whose ways are not our ways, but, as Job found out, God never loses. He declares in Job 38:2, "Who is this that darkens my counsel with words without knowledge?"

However, even when we agree with God's way of salvation, we still have some important issues to think through. What should a church that has not replaced Israel look like, and how do Israel and the church both fit into God's purposes today?

To answer those questions, we need to clear the ground of any false presuppositions, wrong beliefs, or unwholesome prejudice.

Reflecting on this, I was reminded of these words from the book of Hosea, "Ephraim is a trained heifer that loves to thresh; so I will put a yoke on her fair neck. I will drive Ephraim, Judah must plow, and Jacob must break up the ground. Sow righteousness for yourselves, reap the fruit of unfailing love, and break up your unplowed ground; for it is time to seek the Lord, until he comes and showers his righteousness on you."[3]

Unlike garden soil that is easily dug up to plant seeds, unplowed ground is generally hard to turn over. Yet in Hosea's prophecy, the tribes of Israel were to make a formidable plowing team. God promised to provide them with all the power needed to break any ground of deception for the seed of truth to be planted. The fruit of their labor would then be the final harvest of righteousness, which would give glory to God in the heavens and bless His faithful people on earth.

Before the Reformation there was no harvest to be seen. But eventually this became the catalyst for change because Luther's unanswered questions pushed him to seek God outside the box. He did not know where he was heading, or even what he was looking for, but deep down he knew that there was truth to be found out there. His persistence finally led him to new horizons and the radical breakthrough that righteousness was "from first to last by faith."[4]

Five More Theses

Even so, Luther's theses did not go as far as they should have done. I realized I needed to add five more to his ninety-five to clear the ground so that today's church could be what it should be. With trepidation and excitement, I began to write what was to form the basis for the rest of my journey — the five theses that God had opened my eyes to.

Thesis 1: It is a lie that the Church replaced Israel in God's purposes.

Thesis 2: The failure to expose the Great Deception distorted the gospel of the Reformation.

Thesis 3: This deception continues to wound both the church and the Jewish people.

Thesis 4: The truth about God's ongoing purposes for the nation of Israel must stand alongside His purposes for the church.

Thesis 5: The widespread acceptance of this truth will have great consequence for the church and for the salvation of all Israel.

With these five theses nailed in place, it was now possible to plow the hard ground. I started with God's purpose statement for Israel, "I will also make you a light for the Gentiles that you may bring my salvation to the ends of the earth."[5]

God's intention was that Israel would reflect His light into a dark world to the extent that Gentile nations would crave salvation instead of darkness. Just as we get rid of the darkness by switching on the light, Israel was to be the lighting system of the world, and God was to be its power supply.

This traced back to the very first promise that God gave to Abraham, "I will make you into a great nation, and I will bless you; I will make your name great, and you will be a blessing. I will bless those who bless you, and whoever curses you I will curse; and all peoples on earth will be blessed through you."[6]

It was the counterpoint to the story of Babel, when men had sought to raise themselves up by building a tower as high as the heavens.[7] In His anger, God had scattered them and confused them. But with this promise, He had reassured His own people that whether they were to be scattered or confused, He would never give them up.

The promise to Abraham's descendants became more specific through Moses at Sinai, "If you obey me fully and keep my covenant, then out of all nations you will be my treasured possession."[8]

Although they were "the fewest of all peoples,"[9] He anointed them to be "a kingdom of priests and a holy nation."[10]

A Nation Set Apart

God had chosen Israel, a stiff-necked people from the least of all nations, to be uniquely set apart. Israel was to stand out as His example of righteousness in a world that had turned its back on Him. Israel was to express a standard by which His purposes for all the nations might be measured and to be His channel of salvation to the Gentiles. Israel was to be "the apple," the iris of His eye,"[11] the most precious and sensitive part of His very being, the lens through which everything else on earth was to be seen.

This is why God had promised that He would love it with an "everlasting love."[12] He would love Israel as a husband should love his wife,[13] unconditionally and forever, regardless of how it responded.

This is also why He had sworn by His creation that nothing would ever diminish His love for His people.

"He who appoints the sun to shine by day, who decrees the moon and the stars to shine by night, who stirs up the sea so that its waves roar . . . Only if these decrees vanish from my sight . . . will the descendants of Israel ever cease to be a nation before me. Only if the heavens can be measured and the foundations of the earth below be searched out will I reject all the descendants of Israel because of all they have done."[14]

In those days, the heavens were limited to the naked eye. Although there were more stars than could be counted, they were still only numbered in the thousands. Since then, modern astronomy has identified one hundred billion galaxies, including our own Milky Way, which alone contains fifty billion planets. It has become impossible to measure the heavens. God was saying that the revelation of Israel's significance would increase in the same way.

Israel was to be a showpiece to other nations. But if it was to demonstrate to the world blessing for obedience and curse for disobedience, it needed nothing less than a cast iron assurance of His faithfulness. This is why right from the very beginning, God gave Abraham an irrevocable promise, "I will establish my covenant as an everlasting covenant between me and you and your descendants after you."[15]

This covenant was everlasting, even if within it there was to be much ongoing process for Israel.

All of this was prophesied when God changed Jacob's name at the ford of Jabbok. Jacob meant "supplanter," "trickster," or "deceiver." At the end of an all-night wrestling match with him, God renamed Jacob and called him Israel, which in Hebrew meant "he has striven with God."

Jacob refused to let go of his adversary, declaring, "I will not let you go unless you bless me." His opponent then told him that his name was now Israel because he had "struggled with God and with men" and had overcome.[16]

That night, Jacob's character was changed. By daybreak, Israel had slain Jacob the liar, the opportunist, and the usurper. He had clung on for a blessing and was no longer asserting himself over God. Before, he had understood righteousness as something that he ought to have. Now, he wanted it at any price.

This story foretold how God's purpose for Israel was to be outworked. Jacob's descendants would have the same struggle until they chose to cling to God at any cost, and this would be the doorway to their unique calling of being a light to the nations.

But in their struggle, they fell short of God's standards and provoked Him to rebuke them, saying, "My people have committed two sins: They have forsaken me, the spring of living water, and have dug their own cisterns, broken cisterns that cannot hold water. Is Israel a servant, a slave by birth? Why then has he become plunder? Lions have roared: they have growled at him. They have laid waste his land; his towns are burned and deserted."[17]

This was not the roaring of the Lion of Judah but of Satan's cohort of demons who were prowling around like roaring lions "looking for someone to devour."[18]

In the midst of its battle, there was no way out for Israel. It remained God's lighting circuit for the world. Its only option was to be switched on or off. Either way, God would still use it for the outworking of His purposes, but unlike electricity, it would be at the cost of being off rather than on. If Israel distanced itself from God, it would move outside His protection and become easy prey.

However, in His sovereignty, God continued to reveal His purposes to His chosen ones and never ceased to maintain a remnant. Their light may have been scarcely seen on earth, but it was still seen in the heavenly realms, as God reminded Elijah when he despaired of being the only one left, "Yet I reserve seven thousand in Israel - all whose knees have not bowed down to Baal."[19]

God's covenant love was for the entire Jewish people and as much for the unfaithful as for the faithful. When Israel sinned and was exiled to Babylon for seventy years, it was to the whole nation that God said, "For I know the plans I have for you . . . plans to prosper you and not to harm you, plans to give you a hope and a future . . . I will be found by you and will bring you back from captivity. I will gather you from all the nations and places where I have banished you . . . and will bring you back to the place from which I carried you into exile."[20]

Despite having had to discipline Israel severely, God evidently still loved it. Nothing thus far suggested that He had changed His mind. Come what may, it was through Israel that He was going to bring salvation to the world.

The Crucial Question

This raised the crucial question of whether the coming of the Messiah would change this in any way. But four times, Paul's answer in Romans 11 was an emphatic "no." Beginning in verse 1, he said, "Did God reject His people? By no means!" In verse 11, he asserted, "Did they stumble so as to fall beyond recovery? Not at all!" Then in verse 28, he continued, "As far as election is concerned, they are loved on account of the patriarchs." And lastly in verse 29, he concluded, "God's gifts and his call are irrevocable."

Clearly, the coming of Yeshua had not changed Israel's calling. Paul went on to explain how it would be outworked in the future. It would begin with Israel's hardening in part until the fullness of the Gentiles came in and then Israel would experience a softening, which would be nothing less than "life from the dead." This was why he could say "all Israel will be saved."[21] Only at that point would Israel become the light to the nations that God had intended it to be.

All this shows how central the whole of Israel is in the outworking of God's purposes. It illustrates how His overarching plan of salvation goes far beyond the saving of individuals from hell to eternal life. It highlights how serious it is for the Church to usurp Israel's role in God's purposes. And it emphasizes how essential it is for us to understand that God's process for the Jewish people is not about them "coming over to us".

Thus far, my symbolic plow had successfully broken the hard ground, but then it appeared to hit solid rock. Evidently, God equally loved Israel and the church, but for different reasons and in different ways. So how could they simultaneously find fullness of expression in God's plan and purpose? How could they possibly overlap, let alone coexist?

I first wondered why it all seemed so complicated until I suspected that there might be an immense treasure buried deep underneath. A treasure so valuable, so essential, that the devil had worked relentlessly to keep the church from finding it. Without this treasure, it would be oblivious to its true identity and destiny and, therefore, no big threat to him.

I was to discover that this treasure was about the one people of God in two parts, each with its own status and calling, for the One New Man has a testimony of spiritual riches that the devil cannot stand against.

Jewish and Gentile believers have the same spiritual status in Yeshua. "There is neither Jew nor Greek, slave nor free, male nor female"[22] for they are all one in Christ Jesus. However, they do not have the same spiritual calling. In Him, a Jew remains a Jew and a Gentile remains a Gentile just as a woman remains a woman and a man remains a man. Their status is the same, but their calling remains different.

Because "God's gifts and his call are irrevocable,"[23] the calling of a Jew, saved or unsaved, remains the same. His status of being saved through Yeshua or unsaved, however, greatly affects the outworking of his Jewishness.

Together, we are the one people of God, through whom He is outworking His purpose in two different ways. "For he himself is our peace, who has made the two one and has destroyed the barrier, the dividing wall of hostility, by abolishing in his flesh the law with its commandments and regulations. His purpose was to create in himself one new man out of the two, thus making peace, and in this one body to reconcile both of them to God through the cross, by which he put to death their hostility."[24]

When we jointly shine God's light, we will release immense spiritual riches and power into the world.

Right now, it is hard for us to imagine what it will look like, but we are told that it will get easier toward the end. As more of Israel receives Yeshua as its Messiah, the gap will narrow, as it does between a man and a woman when they progressively become one in marriage.

Israel Still the Focus

However, it will still not be about "the Jews coming over to us" because God said, "I will pour out on the house of David and the inhabitants of Jerusalem a spirit of grace and supplication. They will look on me, the one they have pierced, and they will mourn for him as one mourns for an only child, and grieve bitterly for him as one grieves for a firstborn son."[25]

In repentance, many will come to know Yeshua as their Messiah. Then God will sanctify them, "On that day a fountain will be opened to the house of David and the inhabitants of Jerusalem, to cleanse them from sin and impurity."[26]

This will be followed by much persecution, when two-thirds of the population will perish and only one-third will be left, "This third I will bring into the fire; I will refine them like silver and test them like gold."[27]

But then God will rescue them: "A day of the Lord is coming when your plunder will be divided among you. I will gather all the nations to Jerusalem to fight against it . . . Then the Lord will go out and fight against those nations, as he fights in the day of battle. On that day his feet will stand on the Mount of Olives, east of Jerusalem, and the Mount of Olives will be split in two from east to west."[28]

Then He will reveal his glory over all the earth: "On that day living water will flow out of Jerusalem, half to the eastern sea and half to the western sea, in summer and in winter. The Lord will be king over the whole earth. On that day, there will be one Lord, and his name the only name."[29]

Finally, Israel and the nations will worship God together: "The survivors from all the nations that have attacked Jerusalem will go up year after year to worship the King, the Lord Almighty, and to celebrate the Feast of Tabernacles."[30]

Zechariah did not have the words to describe what he was seeing, but he knew that Israel was to be central to future events and was to have a God-given impact on the nations. It would remain "the apple of His eye" through which everything else would be seen.

When hard ground is broken up and the seed is eventually sown, perseverance reaps a harvest. "As the rain and the snow come down from heaven, and do not return to it without watering the earth and making it bud and flourish, so that it yields seed for the sower and bread for the eater, so is my word that goes forth from my mouth. It will not return to me empty, but will accomplish what I desire, and achieve the purpose for which I sent it."[31]

God has called Israel to serve so that the nations might be saved and His righteousness might be displayed. The church's part is to love the Jewish people unconditionally, regardless of whether or not they recognize Yeshua as their Messiah. This is how God has chosen to love them, and there is no better way for us to reflect our appreciation of His love. This is how we truly resonate with His heartbeat and where we will feel it most closely.

To only love them in order to evangelize them is to fall into the same trap as Luther. To love them means respecting their right to reject Yeshua as their Messiah, just as God does. To love them when they do embrace Yeshua as their Messiah is to not demand that they become Gentile as so many of their persecutors did in the Middle Ages. Their Jewish heritage and biblical tradition is a precious blessing to be preserved.

When the church understands what all this means, it will recover the truth of its identity and of its destiny.

CHAPTER 5

Protecting and Nurturing the Truth

I NOW REFLECTED ON WHAT the seed of truth would need to be brought to harvest.

Between sowing and reaping, there is much work to do. It takes moist soil, sunlight, and warmth for seed to germinate. And it takes nurturing and protection for the tender plants to grow.

But the harvest of righteousness will also have to contend with the malevolence of the master destroyer. This is why Yeshua told the story of the man who sowed good seed in his field unawares that his enemy had blighted it with weeds while he was sleeping.[1]

The lie that "God has finished with Israel" has always been Satan's trump card to choke the growth of the church and kill its harvest in the bud.

Surreptitiously, he has sown anti-Semitism as he whispered far and wide, "Did God really say that Israel is still significant?" He has scattered this weed throughout history, gaining the ear of the Reformers and corrupting their theology on the way.

Time passes and circumstances are different, but this lie has retained the same power of persuasion to this day.

Even so, the devil had evidently not bargained that the Jews' return to their land would happen just as was foretold.

"'However, the days are coming' declares the Lord when men will no longer say, 'As surely as the Lord lives, who brought the Israelites up out of Egypt' but they will say 'As surely as the Lord lives, who brought the Israelites up out of the land of the north and out of all the countries where he had banished them.' For I will restore them to the land I gave their forefathers."[2]

This was not about Israel's return from the Babylonian exile because Babylon was southeast and not north. The prophecy spoke of a much greater return of Israel, which was to be from many countries, not just from one. The Jews were to come back from the four corners of the earth where they had been scattered. As Michael Elkins describes, "They came from all of Europe, they came from Russia, from the United States, South Africa, Canada, Argentina, Australia, Iraq, Turkey, Iran, Tunisia, from the Atlas mountains in Morocco. They came from places where most people hardly imagined that there could be Jews — from India, China, from the Hadramout of Aden, from the mountains and jungles of Ethiopia . . . They came from forty two countries, from Western cultures, Eastern cultures, from tribal cultures as primitive as the Stone Age. They were monogamous, polygamous. They were doctors, lawyers, merchants, goldsmiths, witch doctors, goat herders. They hunted with blowpipes, with clubs, bows and arrows. They were Jews, all of them Jews."[3]

On May 14, 1948, the fulfillment of Jeremiah's prophecy was given its official stamp of legitimacy when David Ben Gurion declared that the state of Israel was born.

After two thousand years, the Jews came home, and over six decades on, they are still returning to the land. Whether the world accepts it or not, Israel's survival as an identifiable people is unparalleled in all history. Today, despite the raging frustration and envious coveting of its surrounding enemies, Israel survives and thrives. It is largely secular, yet the promise of its future righteousness still stands. And the devil's lie that the remaining prophecies will not be fulfilled literally is gradually being disproved.

However, having successfully coerced the Church into believing that it has replaced Israel, nothing will deter him from still propagating his poisonous weeds wherever he can. He does it covertly by harnessing the inherent fears of nations to promote anti-Semitism and overtly by fanning anti-Zionism in the corridors of power. The devil can see that the fields are white and ready for harvest and knows that his time will soon be up.

He is running scared because the harvest of righteousness is a much greater threat to him than the salvation of however many individuals. As the time of the end approaches, so does his final destination in the pit of hell. But he will not go quietly and until then will cause as much chaos amongst believers as he can.

We are seeing with our own eyes what the prophets only saw from afar. The rebirth of the Hebrew nation is the first fruit of the final harvest, the beginning of the end when all things will be made new. As God's chosen custodians of this unprecedented season, we have both an immense privilege and a commensurate accountability. We are the ones called by God to protect His precious seed of righteousness from the weed-sowing tactics of the adversary. Our tasks are to resist the devil[4] and to take our stand against his evil schemes[5] so that he does not outwit us.[6] In practice, it means rescinding the Great Deception, reversing its curse, and restoring the distortion of the gospel.

There is no time to lose.

Rescinding the Great Deception

Rescinding the Great Deception is about exposing it and breaking its power. It is about storming its stronghold to destroy it in the name of Yeshua. Casual praying is not enough because this lie has been in force for over two thousand years. It needs the strategic intercession of God's mighty prayer warriors.

The Great Deception has to be individually renounced and replaced with the truth. For that, we first need to check our own hearts because we might ourselves be deceived without knowing it.

The mistake is to believe that anti-Semitism is only about hating the Jewish people. But love is an active word that has no room for indifference or aloofness. In fact, Yeshua warned us that "he who is not with me is against me, and he who does not gather with me scatters."[7]

The hatred of God's chosen people can be so subtle and insidious that it takes the power of the Holy Spirit to unearth it from within us. However, when we humbly ask God to examine our hearts, like David, we have the assurance that He will reveal any offensive way in us and lead us to repentance.[8] When we have repented, we then need to intentionally step into the truth.

This begins by accepting that today's state of Israel is not an accident of history but an act of God's grace and sovereignty in the outworking of His final purposes.

Paul urges us to be transformed by the renewing of our minds immediately after telling us about God's continuing purposes for Israel.[9] This encourages us to see salvation through the great lens of God's choice of Israel, instead of the microscopic lens of our own salvation. It also exhorts us to be humble about being grafted into Israel and having its Jewish Messiah within us.

With this perspective in mind, it is easier to see that we "do not support the root, but the root supports us."[10] We can better appreciate that the demonization of the Jews touches the apple of God's eye and dishonors Yeshua. And we can better understand that if we criticize Israel, we become the devil's advocate, injuring ourselves in the process.[11]

This perspective also enables us to choose to love Israel regardless of its failings, simply because God first chose to love it. It does not mean that we have to blindly support Israel's every move in order to stand with those with whom we share God's covenant and promises. We simply have to learn from Noah's sons how to avert our eyes from Israel's nakedness, just as God does with us.[12]

Amidst biased media reports, we need to engage with the inner battle and confusion going on in the minds and hearts of fellow believers regarding Israel. If we do this with respect and love, we will be in a far better position to resist the lies of the devil.

If in any way this affronts our thinking, we can remind ourselves that God's ways are higher than ours and that He has determined how and through whom He will outwork His end-time scenario.

"Oh the depth of the riches of the wisdom and knowledge of God! How unsearchable his judgments, and his paths beyond tracing out! Who has known the mind of the Lord? Or who has been his counselor? Who has ever given to God, that God should repay him?"[13]

REVERSING THE CURSE

To reverse is to go back in the opposite direction. It is only when we chose to actively bless the Jewish people that the curse brought in by the Great Deception can be turned around. God gives us freedom to decide whether or not we will, but He warns us that if we don't, it can have serious consequences in our lives. As He said to Abraham, "I will make you into a great nation, and I will bless you; I will make your name great and you will be a blessing. I will bless those who bless you, and whoever curses you I will curse; and all peoples on earth will be blessed through you."[14]

These dynamics are clearly outplayed in the lives of individuals. When Yeshua healed the sick servant, He was blessing back the Roman soldier who had built the Jews a synagogue.[15] By contrast, when Haman and Hitler sought to exterminate the Jews, one was hung on the gallows and the other shot himself. Luther himself died soon after writing his hateful tome *Concerning the Jews and Their Lies*.

There are many telling examples of the rise and fall of nations as a result of whether they blessed or cursed the Jewish people. For instance, after it expulsed the Jews in the fifteenth century, Spain ceased to be a dominant world power. Yet the primitive country of Turkey became a world empire after its Sultan welcomed them in.

When Pharaoh refused to let the children of Israel go after four hundred years of slavery in Egypt, his nation suffered ten life-threatening plagues that included the death of all its firstborn sons. And when he pursued his anti-Semitic policy as far as the Red Sea, he never came home. Today, Egypt's economy depends on the distant memory of its former prestige, which now lies in the dust of its temples and pyramids.

Rome, the mightiest empire of all times, prided itself on its bloody destruction of Jerusalem. But its fame rapidly declined in the following centuries, and today it is just one of many tourist destinations. In the same way, the British Empire went into decline after it reneged on its promises to Israel made in the 1917 Balfour Declaration. Of course, these could all be random coincidences, but they fit remarkably well with God's prophetic warnings.

As far as blessing the Jews, the Gentile Church is indisputably in arrears, and yet if it turns around and recognizes that "salvation is from the Jews,"[16] it can still reverse the curse and make restitution.

We Gentiles have been entrusted with the awesome mandate of making "Israel envious"[17] by being "salt and light" wherever we live and work. We have been commissioned to intercede for the Jews until they can say of Yeshua, "Blessed is he who comes in the name of the Lord."[18] Informed, yet relying on the Holy Spirit, we are to pray for the peace of Jerusalem[19] so that in the midst of its confusion, it may encounter the Prince of Peace. And our love can be translated into actions by blessing Israel in material ways, such as giving the much-needed practical support to its emerging Messianic congregations.[20] When the Church does all of this and more, the curse will be truly reversed.

Restoring the Distortion of the Gospel

The father of lies has misrepresented the gospel by luring the body of believers away from its Jewish roots. Bending the truth as he did in Eden, he has managed to convince Gentile believers that its original Hebraic context was irrelevant. Restoring the gospel from the distortion of the Great Deception will leave us dissatisfied with partial truth and make us hungry for it as a whole.

Like the entrance to a magnificent building, our personal salvation is only the doorway to God's greater plan of salvation. We have to go through and beyond the door if we are to discover the spaciousness inside.

When we do, we gain a better grasp of what we have been saved from because before our adoption, we were nothing less than "separate from Christ, excluded from citizenship in Israel and foreigners to the covenants of the promise, without hope and without God in the world."[21]

With this in mind, we also gain a clearer perspective of what we have received through Israel because "theirs is the adoption as sons; theirs the divine glory, the covenants, the receiving of the law, the temple worship and the promises."[22] We are better able to measure how far we have come from and how near we "have been brought through the blood of Christ."[23]

We can grasp how much more the blood of Yeshua has achieved beyond redeeming us from our sins as we fully enter into the adoption, the glory, the covenants, and the promises that were made to Israel. And we can discover how we "are Abraham's seed, and heirs according to the promise."[24]

As those who have been given spiritual citizenship with Israel, we can feel genuinely at home in the house of God. We can truly be coheirs with Israel and coworkers with God, protecting and nurturing the harvest until it is finally brought in.

If we enter through the doorway to salvation but venture no further, we will miss out on the extravagance of God's promises. Our understanding of His greater purposes will remain partial, incomplete, and distorted. The most we will appreciate is the small overlap between the church and Israel and the tiny percentage of Messianic believers in Israel today.[25] But if we do venture further, we will see the miracle of the ever-growing Messianic community in Israel and the rest of the world.

The prophets tell us that growing pressure on the nation of Israel from all sides will cause its people to genuinely cry out to God. In their desperation, many will turn to Yeshua and acknowledge Him as their awaited Messiah. Israel will align itself to God's purposes and fulfill its mission to be a light to the nations, and the Lord will be king over the whole earth.[26]

Finally, the worldwide celebration of the end-time harvest will go up from earth to heaven as God showers righteousness from heaven to earth. The fullness of salvation will be such that it will reflect indescribable glory to the only true God, and the devil will not be able to do anything about it.

This is the context, this is the perspective, and this is the awe-inspiring vision that takes us beyond our personal salvation.

CHAPTER 6

Preparing for the Harvest of Righteousness

AT THIS POINT IN my journey, I began to think about how those who escape the Great Deception might play their part in preparing for the final harvest.

Only crops ripened by the sun can be harvested. In the same way, the final harvest will have to be ready to glean. Its ripening will come when the "fullness of the Gentiles" shines on Israel, producing a death-to-life experience and opening it up to salvation. Then "all Israel shall be saved," just as Paul said would happen. "The deliverer will come from Zion; he will turn godlessness away from Jacob. And this is my covenant with them when I take away their sins."[1]

But first, the Gentile body of believers will have to enter into a fullness that surpasses anything to do with its numbers. "The fullness of the Gentiles" is often wrongly translated as "the full number of the Gentiles."[2] It implies that Israel can only begin to soften for the harvest when Gentile believers reach a certain number. But here the word "fullness" comes from the Greek word "pleroma," which means completeness. It alludes to a wholeness that far exceeds anything that can be quantified with numbers.

It is demonstrated in the way Paul that used "pleroma" elsewhere in his letters "The earth is the Lord's, and all its fullness (pleroma)."[3] "For in Christ all the fullness (pleroma) of the Deity lives in bodily form."[4] ". . . which is his body, the fullness (pleroma) of him who fills everything in every way."[5]

Had he just wanted to refer to the full number of the Gentiles, Paul would have used the word "arithmou," which he used when he spoke about the number of the Israelites being "like the sand by the sea."[6]

Although cumbersome, a fairer interpretation of what he actually said would therefore sound like this:

"Israel has experienced a hardening in part until there is

- the full number of Gentile believers ordained by God to be saved
- the full representation of every tribe, language, people and nation ordained by God to be saved
- the full understanding that the Gentile believers are grafted into Israel, as it fulfills God's purpose in His greater final plan of salvation."

However, most of the current translations do not give the fullness of the message that Paul wanted to communicate.

When Yeshua spoke about the signs of the end of the age, He warned that Jerusalem would be trampled on by the Gentiles "until the times of the Gentiles are fulfilled."[7]

We Gentiles will only value our strategic role in the final scenario when we grasp the significance of the "fullness of the Gentiles." Only then will we be able to do our part in halting the "trampling" of Jerusalem.

This has immense implications. Resisting the devil's attempts to thwart the coming harvest is not enough. We need to be clean reflectors, accurately aligned toward God's truth, if we are to shine His radiant light on Israel.

To sabotage this, the enemy is determined to keep the Church in a bubble, unaware of what is at stake. He is also intent on deflecting every believer away from the whole truth of salvation. This is the strategy he practiced on Martin Luther, regarding where the emphasis should go on his great breakthrough verse "a righteousness that is by faith from first to last."[8]

Luther's emphasis on "how" to receive salvation introduced the idea of a gospel that was primarily about a personal relationship with God. It resurrected the truth of salvation that had been dormant through generations of religious confusion, and it opened the way to the salvation of countless millions of people. However, if he had gone one step further and put a similar emphasis on "what" faith was for, history might have been very different.

In missing the truth that personal right standing with God is only part of the much greater picture, Luther did not embrace the whole biblical view of righteousness, which expresses the heart of God.

Yeshua never taught that we should seek first our personal salvation but that we should seek first His Father's "kingdom and His righteousness."[9] We do need to be individually made right with Him; nevertheless, our lives are to be about God's kingdom and not ours. Any other view leads us to a "me-centered" Gospel and a distorted understanding of Yeshua's full atonement on the cross. Any other view also deviates us from the truth that Israel remains God's chosen channel to bring light to the nations at the end of the age.

The Prior Filling of Gentile Believers

We do not know the depth of spiritual battle that Luther endured just to get as far as he did, nor do we know what deflected him from getting to the whole truth of the fullness of salvation. We do know, however, that although he came close to it, he ended up a very long way from it.

What seemed to be just a matter of emphasis actually ended up legitimizing anti-Semitism and causing the divide between the Church and Israel, with terrible collateral consequences. Because of it, the church will have to face its spiritual tunnel vision and regain God's eternal perspective if it is to be involved in the final harvest. It will have to check its theological blind spots to see that Israel has never ceased to be the apple of God's eye. When it does, it will quickly recognize the nearness of its own fullness in the current softening of the Jewish people.

The Reformers who succeeded Luther followed his trend. Calvin added his own brand to the idea of an exclusively personal salvation. He did not believe in a literal end-time rule of Yeshua, calling it "fiction" in his Institutes saying that it was "too childish either to need or to be worth a refutation."[10]

Regarding the disciples' question about the timing of Israel's restoration and Yeshua's reply that only the Father knew the answer, Calvin commented, "There were as many errors as words in the apostles' question . . . it proved how bad scholars they were under so good a master."[11]

Another time he declared that "when Jesus said 'you shall receive power,' he was admonishing them of their imbecility."[12]

His views, intertwined with the thread of replacement theology, were soon woven into the very fabric of the Reformation. They left the Church with a legacy of deception, which has bound and weakened it ever since.

But like replacement theology, these were actually centuries-old presumptions just given a facelift. Calvin was only building on what had already been taught erroneously before him.

It had begun in the second century with Aristobulus and Philo, who fused together Hebrew and Greek thinking to interpret scripture. From them to Origen, to Augustine, to the Reformers, and to this day, it has lead to great aberrations in Christian thinking.

For example, in his book *The City of God*, Augustine said that the abyss, destined for Satan in the millennium, was not a literal place. "By the abyss is meant the countless multitude of the wicked whose hearts are unfathomably deep in malignity against the Church of God." He also believed that the binding of Satan in the abyss was about "his being unable to seduce the Church" and already a reality of the present age.[13]

Beyond such aberrations, the practice of allegorical interpretation provided a neat way around uncomfortable passages of scripture and especially those of Revelation, which at one point Luther did not even recognize as apostolic writing.[14] Most importantly, it became a very useful tool to avoid explaining the literal role of Israel in God's end-time scenario.

With this mind-set, end-time prophecies were to the Reformers no more than allegorical stories. Following the footsteps of others, they emphatically taught that the physical kingdom of Israel had been superseded by the spiritual kingdom of heaven. This treatment of scripture disempowered its truth and diminished its impact on the body of believers. The inspired symbolism used in the Word was disabled, and its anointed messages were disconnected. It left the Church with a bland imagery which failed to bring the incisiveness that God intended.

Crucially, the link between Yeshua as the Passover Lamb and Yeshua as the Primal Lion got lost in the process. Instead, an image of weakness rather than meekness was projected, eroding the authority and strength Yeshua spoke about when He said, "From the days of John the Baptist until now, the kingdom of heaven has been forcefully advancing, and forceful men lay hold of it."[15]

The devastating result is that today's dumbed-down Church is failing to trust in the literal truth of the Word of God. Most preachers will merely speak about going to heaven when we die. Braver ones will dare to mention in passing that we have been saved from hell. Some might get a bee in their bonnet about the rapture being either before or after the tribulation. But few have the boldness to speak enthusiastically about what we have been saved for, which is to reign quite literally in the kingdom of the Lion of the tribe of Judah as scripture says we will. Revelation 5:9–10 declares, "You are worthy to take the scroll and to open its seals, because you were slain, and with your blood you purchased men for God from every tribe and language and people and nation. You have made them to be a kingdom and priests to serve our God, and they will reign on earth."

If we believe that we were literally saved through the shed blood of the Lion-Lamb, then we must also believe that we are literally destined to a reign of righteousness. To interpret the first part of this verse literally and the second part allegorically is illogical and inconsistent. It is either all true or not true at all.

The Paschal Lamb and the Primal Lion

The heavenly song of "the living creatures and the twenty four elders"[16] inspires us to shift our focus from our own salvation to Yeshua's end-time reign, and to expand our understanding of what took place on the cross. The me-centered gospel that came out of the Reformation essentially sees the cross as the place where Yeshua bore my sins and atoned for me. However, John's revelation gives us a very different perspective. "And I saw a mighty angel proclaiming in a loud voice 'Who is worthy to break open the seals and open the scroll?' But no one in heaven or on earth could open the scroll and even look inside it. I wept and wept because no one was found who was worthy to open the scroll or look inside. Then one of the elders said to me, 'Do not weep! See, the Lion of the tribe of Judah, the root of David, has triumphed. He is able to open the scroll and its seven seals.'"

The Lion of the tribe of Judah was the most magnificent and poignant of revelations. Yet it left John gasping. When he looked up to see who had triumphed, he did not see the Lion, he saw a Lamb which appeared "as if it had been slain."[17]

Only the Lion-Lamb was found worthy to take the scroll and open its seals. As He opened them one at a time, the revelation of future salvation and judgment was released on the earth.

It was followed by an even greater revelation of the divine plan. This was to complete what began when God created man in His own image and placed him on earth to be fruitful and multiply. And although we are not told why, it transpired that all of this hinged on the Lion of Judah's willingness to become the slain Lamb who would die on a human cross.

His victory there was not only over the devil but also over the entire host of evil spiritual powers. Colossians 2:15 explains how "having disarmed the powers and authorities, he made a public spectacle of them, triumphing over them by the cross." This was the long-prophesied triumph of both the Lion of the tribe of Judah and the root of David. Understanding the significance of those two titles is key to the church's ability to triumph ahead of the final victory.

The five words "of the tribe of Judah" came from the blessing that Jacob, who became Israel, gave to each of his twelve sons before he died. By blessing his sons, he was effectively blessing the twelve future tribes of Israel. He gave an appropriate blessing to each, but he specifically said to Judah, "You are a lion's cub, O Judah; you return from the prey, my son. Like a lion he crouches and lies down, like a lioness — who dares to rouse him? The scepter will not depart from Judah, nor the ruler's staff from between his feet, until he comes to whom it belongs and the obedience of nations is his."[18]

These prophetic words pointed to the final triumph of the Lion of the tribe of Judah. Just as a lion chooses a territory to establish his rule, so it was to be with the heavenly Lion. He singled out the nation of Israel and declared his lordship over it. Then through it, He chose to reveal Himself and outwork His purposes.

Jacob was also prophesying that a royal line would come through the descendants of Judah's tribe. It would be traced through its kings all the way down to the Lion-Lamb who was to be born as man.

The royal line of David, son of Jesse, was then compared to a fallen tree out of which a new tree would spring forth to restore his kingly rule. Isaiah's glorious prophecy of the promised Messianic kingdom added that "He will not judge by what he sees with his eyes, or decide by what he hears with his ears; but with righteousness he will judge the needy, with justice he will give decisions for the poor of the earth. He will strike the earth with the rod of his mouth; with the breath of his lips he will slay the wicked. Righteousness will be his belt and faithfulness the sash round his waist. They will neither harm nor destroy on all my holy mountain, for the earth will be full of the knowledge of the Lord as the waters cover the sea. In that day, the root of Jesse will stand as a banner for the peoples; the nations will rally to him and his place of rest will be glorious."[19]

Right now, we only have a mere glimpse of what is to come but this glimpse is enough to point us to a reality in which we have an awesome and unprecedented part to play.

"Then the sovereignty, power and greatness of the kingdoms under the whole heaven will be handed over to the saints, the people of the Most High. His kingdom will be an everlasting kingdom, and all rulers will worship and obey him."[20]

"See, the Lord is coming with thousands upon thousands of his holy ones to judge everyone, and to convict all the ungodly of all the ungodly acts they have done in the ungodly way, and all the harsh words ungodly sinners have spoken against him."[21]

"Do you not know the saints will judge the world? And if you are to judge the world, are you not competent to judge trivial cases? Do you not know that we will judge angels?"[22]

In this extraordinary final harvest, the Lion-Lamb will exercise as much force as necessary to eliminate all unrighteousness. Following a brief release of Satan before his final destruction, a new heaven and a new earth will become the glorious dwellings of all those who have been washed in the blood of the Lamb.

Although we can only see these future events as if "through a glass, darkly"[23] we must decide whether they are literal or allegorical. If we choose to believe the latter, we have nothing to prepare for, and we can just stay in our comfortable bubble for as long as it may last. If we choose the former, we need to get ready to receive God's promised fullness for the outworking of his purposes. There is no middle ground.

A Single Question

It became clear to me that the enigma of "complete the reformation" could be condensed into a single question. What had initially seemed so open-ended had finally narrowed down to one specific challenge, a question to the church as a whole and to each believer in particular, "Is your vision based on the lie or on the Lion?"

They did not see it this way, or even see it at all, but this should have been the Reformers' greatest yardstick. They stormed the stronghold of salvation by works and achieved an indisputable breakthrough. But when they approached the stronghold that lay behind it, they avoided it rather than addressed it. This is why the Reformation remained so critically incomplete, and why, in the face of an apparent wipe out, the devil retained his power to deceive even the elect.

Calvin, like Luther, came so near and yet ended so far away in his endeavor to establish a visible city of God. For a season, legislation reinforced by stringent inquisitions enabled him to transform Geneva into a city free from immorality, but it was flawed from the beginning. It was not founded on the fullness of the gospel because it did not include the final vision of the roaring Lion of the tribe of Judah. Consequently, it did not bring in the fullness of the Gentiles as it should have done.

This was the inevitable outcome of rejecting God's ongoing purpose for Israel and teaching that end-time prophecies were no more than allegories.

This story is not just history. It created an enormous vacuum that has had a devastating effect on the Church's mind-set regarding its identity, destiny, and testimony to this day.

But this does not have to define the Church any more if it chooses to embrace its fullness, to get out of its Gentile bubble, and to step into the miracles that God promised to those who are grafted into Israel. Isaiah 62:1-2 declares, "For Zion's sake I will not keep silent, for Jerusalem's sake I will not remain quiet, till her righteousness shines out like the dawn, her salvation like a blazing torch. The nations will see your righteousness, and all kings your glory; you will be called by a new name that the mouth of the Lord will bestow."

When this happens, Israel will see and understand this ancient promise, "'How can I give you up Ephraim? How can I hand you over, Israel? They will follow the Lord; he will roar like a lion. When he roars, his children will come trembling from the west. They will come trembling like birds from Egypt, like doves from Assyria. I will settle them in their homes', declares the Lord."[24]

And when this fully happens, those who escape the Great Deception will also see and understand.

I finally understood that although at the Reformation the Great Deception should have been exposed and halted, it was not. It was regenerated rather than reformed. Worst of all, it was given a new momentum, sufficient to carry it forward to this day.

But it is not too late for the people of God. Today the Lion is roaring. He is calling us to heed His warning and escape the Great Deception. He is calling us to roar with Him, to stand with Israel, and to prepare for the harvest of all harvests.

Let the Lion roar.

FOOTNOTE 1

What's Wrong with Replacement Theology?

REPLACEMENT THEOLOGY, OR SUPERSESSIONISM, alleges that when Israel rejected its Messiah, God saw fit to transfer His covenants and promises to the Church. From then on, the Church was deemed to be the "new and improved" version of Israel, which superseded Israel in God's purposes.

The New Covenant promised explicitly to Israel was then appropriated by the Church,[1] and so were the promises of its re-gathering, restoration, and deliverance, which were conveniently spiritualized. Israel was no longer regarded as the chosen nation and no longer credited with a specific role or future. The name "Israel" given to Jacob now referred to all those who had received the New Covenant, and Galatians 3:29, which speaks of being

Abraham's seed if we belong to Christ, became the proof text for the proponents of this theology.

Believers became "heirs according to the promise" by direct transfer rather than by being grafted in. To add insult to injury, the Church appropriated the title "the Israel of God" from Galatians 6:16 and did the same with "the apple of God's eye."[2] The nation of Israel was considered to be no more than the necessary seed of a future Church, which would by itself restore God's forthcoming dominion described in Malachi 1:11.

Texts out of context became pretexts to support replacement theology, such as Matthew 21:23, where Yeshua says that the kingdom of God would be given to those who would best produce its fruit. Romans 2:28-29 was interpreted to say that being a Jew referred to an inward disposition, and Galatians 3:28 became proof that the words "Jews" and "Gentiles" were obsolete since we are all one in Christ.

The absurd outcome was that the Church was supposed to now be the spiritual Israel, whilst Israel, when written in the New Testament, was supposed to mean the Church. This utterly overlooked the Hebraic context of scripture with its two thousand five hundred references to Israel and to the Israelites. It was also in complete contrast to what was written in the New Testament about the Jewishness of our faith.

Apart from Luke, Yeshua's followers and the writers of the Old and the New Testaments were all Jewish.

Peter's sermon at the Jewish feast of Pentecost, when the body of believers was born and three thousand Jews were converted, would have meant little to a Gentile audience. According to Acts 2:46, the first disciples met regularly at the temple, which generally did not include the Gentiles. And in Acts 7, when he made his defense before the high priest, Stephen covered the entire Jewish history of Israel because of its relevance to his faith in Yeshua.

When Paul arrived in Jerusalem, the Jewish believers said to him, "You see, brother, how many thousands of Jews have believed, and all of them are zealous for the law."[3] He attended the synagogue regularly, kept kosher throughout his life,[4] identified himself as a Jew,[5] and even circumcised Timothy, who traveled with him.[6]

It is therefore implausible to claim that God has done away with Israel, with the Jews, and with the Jewish roots of our faith.

The erroneous position of replacement theology is flagrant in several other ways.

1. It downgrades scripture.
    a. It works back from its assumptions to make the unconditional nature of God's covenant[7] conditional.
    b. It reduces the literal promises to Israel to allegories.
    c. It greatly manipulates explicit scriptures such as "Did God reject his people? By no means!"[8] "God's gifts

and his call are irrevocable,"[9] and "Salvation is from the Jews."[10]

2. It generates aberrations through its inconsistencies.
   a. It implies that Israel needs to be grafted into the Church, whereas it is the Gentile body of believers which needs to recognize that it is grafted into Israel.[11]
   b. It interprets Israel or Israelite seventy-four times in the New Testament to mean Church or Christian, rendering many of the verses absolutely meaningless.
   c. It ignores the fact that in what is commonly called the Old Testament, the one and only reference to the New Covenant is given to Israel.[12]

3. It engenders ambiguity.
   a. God's rejection of Israel implies by default that He can reject individual believers and even the body of believers as a whole.
   b. The Church's usurping of God's promises makes the prophesied rebirth of the nation of Israel and its miraculous sixty plus years survival an unprecedented anomaly of history.
   c. It confuses the distinction between the identical status of all believers, Jew and Gentile, and their different callings.

4. It impoverishes its followers.
    a. It discourages believers from drawing the "nourishing sap" of the Jewish roots of the faith[13] which then disempowers the church.
    b. It disinclines believers from interceding for Israel and Jerusalem[14] and robs them from looking ahead to the outworking of end-time prophecies.
    c. It distances believers from God by causing them to dishonor the Jews who are still "the apple of his eye." In not loving those He loves, they effectively sin against Him and become vulnerable to falling away.[15]

FOOTNOTE 2

Hasn't Jesus Fulfilled Everything?

FULFILLMENT THEOLOGY IS A relatively recent variant of replacement theology with one significant addition. It introduces an intermediate stage to the direct transfer of the covenants and promises from Israel to the Church. All the promises are deemed to have been completely fulfilled by Jesus, who was able to give them to the Church by representing the true Israel on the cross.

It uses proof texts taken out of context as objections to Israel retaining a role in God's purposes, such as "For no matter how many promises God has made, they are 'Yes' in Christ,"[1] and "Since we have a great high priest who has gone through the heavens, Jesus the Son of God."[2]

Fulfillment theology is sometimes explained with the hourglass analogy of a wide Israel narrowing down to Jesus and then spreading out to the Church. Its advocates claim that it is not replacement theology, but its practical implications are identical. In fact, although it might appear softer, it actually adds further flaws.

- If Yeshua literally became Israel, how could He have fulfilled the promise of a return to the land without ever having been exiled to the four corners of the earth?
- Paul spoke in Romans 11:15 of an ongoing "remnant chosen by grace" without saying that this remnant shrank down to only one in Yeshua. Indeed, scripture suggests quite the opposite.[3]
- The hourglass picture does not fit with the olive tree analogy of Romans 11.

The promises cannot have all been fulfilled in Yeshua when some are yet to be fulfilled at His second coming. For example, in Luke 21:24, He said that Jerusalem will be trodden down by the Gentiles until the times of the Gentiles have been fulfilled. In Acts 3:21, Peter declared that Yeshua must stay in heaven until the time comes for God to restore everything. Paul also wrote in Romans 11:25 that unbelieving Jews will remain hardened until the fullness of the Gentiles has come and, in 1 Corinthians 15:25, that Yeshua must reign until all His enemies are under His feet.

Yeshua fulfilled many promises at his first coming, but if he had fulfilled all the promises, why would He need to come again? And where is the complete fulfillment of those promises to be seen today?

FOOTNOTE 3

What Happened to the Law?

THE MAJOR THRUST BEHIND replacement and fulfillment theology is that the new has completely replaced the old. The view that the Church has replaced Israel then leads to the parallel view that grace has completely replaced the law.

This is then the basis for interpreting verses such as "You are not under law, but under grace"[1] and "Do not think I have come to abolish the Law or the Prophets; I have not come to abolish them but to fulfill them."[2]

However, to reckon that Yeshua superseded the law is a slippery slope to all sorts of contradictions about the nature of the gospel and how we may then behave.

So, for example, if the law has been replaced, why are parts of the Ten Commandments included in the constitutions of many governments today? And if the law does not matter, why does Paul tell us to uphold it?[3]

To resolve these questions, we need a clear understanding of the Old Testament so that we can distinguish between what became obsolete, what remained, and what was new.

To engage with the continuity and the distinctiveness of the two Testaments, it helps to think of them this way, "the New is in the Old concealed, the Old is in the New revealed." It is also more accurate to call them the Older and the Newer Testaments as it gives a stronger basis to explore God's law and His ongoing purposes for Israel.

The five great covenants of scripture are referred to in both Testaments, but each have a different outcome.[4]

They are as follows:

- The Noahic Covenant
- The Abrahamic Covenant
- The Mosaic Covenant
- The Davidic Covenant
- The Messianic Covenant

Immediately after the flood, God gave Noah a covenant that was for the whole human race and was totally unconditional.

"As long as the earth endures, seed time and harvest, cold and heat, summer and winter, day and night will never cease."[5] This, as we know, has not changed because to this day, the sun rises and the rain falls as much on the unrighteous as on the righteous.[6]

By contrast, the covenant given to Abraham was specific to his descendants through Jacob.

"I will make you into a great nation and I will bless you; I will make you great, and you will be a blessing. I will bless those who bless you, and whoever curses you I will curse; and all peoples on earth will be blessed through you."[7]

"I will establish my covenant as an everlasting covenant between me and you and your descendants after you for generations to come."[8]

This covenant was reiterated to Isaac.

"I will make your descendants as numerous as the stars in the sky and will give them all these lands, and through your offspring all nations on earth will be blessed."[9]

The circumcision of every Jewish male was God's only condition, and this covenant was never revoked. In fact, in the Newer Testament, Paul wrote in Hebrews 6:13–18, "When God made his promise to Abraham, since there was no one greater than him to swear by, he swore by himself, saying, 'I will surely bless you and give you many descendants.' And so after waiting patiently, Abraham received what was promised."

Men swear by someone greater than themselves, and the oath confirms what is said and puts an end to all argument. "Because God wanted to make the unchanging nature of his purpose very clear to the heirs of what was promised, he confirmed it with an oath. God did this so that, by two unchangeable things in which it is impossible for God to lie, we who have fled to take hold of the hope offered to us may be greatly encouraged."

The Mosaic Covenant set out in Exodus and Leviticus was different again.[10] In Galatians 3:17–19, Paul explains it this way, "What I mean is this: the law, introduced 430 years later, does not set aside the covenant previously established by God and thus do away with the promise. For if the inheritance depends on the law, then it no longer depends on a promise; but God in his grace gave it to Abraham through a promise.

What then was the purpose of the law? It was added because of transgressions until the Seed to whom the promise referred had come."

The covenant made to Moses was therefore only a temporary addition and was separate to the one made to Abraham.

But unlike the previous ones, the covenant made to David was eternal. It is yet to be completely fulfilled through his offspring as promised in 1 Chronicles 17:14, "I will set him over my house and my kingdom for ever, his throne will be established for ever."

The fifth and final covenant was the Messianic Covenant. "'The time is coming' declares the Lord 'when I will make a new covenant with the house of Israel and with the house of Judah. It will not be like the covenant I made with their forefathers when I took them by the hand to lead them out of Egypt, because they broke my covenant, although I was a husband to them' declares the Lord."[11]

So across the five great covenants, the only changes were within the Mosaic law, which contained the civil, the ceremonial, the health, and the moral law. These temporary laws, given for the sake of structure and order, are the only ones to have been done away with under the New Covenant, except for a few health and moral laws. Structure and order are now to be found in Yeshua, who sets His people free from the bondage of legalism.

This means that "the law is only a shadow of the good things that are coming,"[12] and "Christ is the end of the law"[13] refers to the Mosaic law.

Therefore, the accurate interpretation of "you are not under law, but under grace" refers to the ending of legalism but not the ending of the law. Yeshua redefined the law as active obedience to His Father. He also taught His disciples to follow His example and declared in John 15:14 and 17, "You are my friends if you do what I command . . . This is my command . . . Love each other."

Later in 1 Corinthians 9:21, Paul said, "I am not free from God's law but I am under Christ's law," and told the believers in Galatians 6:2, "Carry each other's burdens, and in this way you will fulfill the law of Christ."

This clearly proves that Yeshua did not supersede the principle of the law. The law had implied that righteousness was attainable through obedience, but when Yeshua embraced the law, he raised the bar even higher. No one could ever reach this height except through His sacrifice.

This way, He set the scene for His final rule and reign when all will know, in the words of Psalm 19:7, that "the law of the Lord is perfect."

FOOTNOTE 4

Whose Land Is It Really?

THE QUESTION OF WHO owns the land claimed by the state of Israel is extremely controversial and provokes much political and legal debate across the nations.[1] The media's focus on the Israeli-Palestinian conflict is out of all proportion to the rest of the news. The United Nations has passed more resolutions against Israel than against any other nation. And although it constitutes only one six-hundredth of the surrounding Arab territories, it is fiercely disputed. Much has been written and said, many opinions have been aired, but the question remains. Who owns the land?

Our conclusion will depend on what we consider to be the starting point of the conflict, whether it is rooted in ancient history, recent history, or both.

According to God's promise to Abram, the land was an intrinsic part of his everlasting covenant. Genesis 12:7 says, "The

Lord appeared to Abram and said 'To your offspring I will give this land.'"

In Genesis 13:14, God declared to Abram, "Lift up your eyes from where you are and look north, south, east and west. All the land that you see I will give to you and your offspring forever."

In Genesis 15:18–21, God promised Abram, "To your descendants I give this land, from the river of Egypt to the great river, the Euphrates — the land of the Kenites, Kenizzites, Kadmonites, Hittites, Perizzites, Rephaites, Amorites, Canaanites, Girgashites and Jebusites."

In Genesis 17:7–8, God also promised to Abram, "I will establish my covenant as an everlasting covenant between me and you and your descendants after you for the generations to come, to be your God and the God of your descendants after you. The whole land of Canaan, where you are now an alien, I will give as an everlasting possession to you and your descendants after you; and I will be their God."

God extended this promise to Jacob on the same basis as He had to Abraham and Isaac.[2] Most importantly He did it soon after changing his name to Israel. Paul endorsed its ongoing validity by saying in Romans 11:28–29 that the Jews are still "loved on account of the patriarchs, for God's gifts and his call are irrevocable."

The land was the most prominent gift to the patriarchs. If the Jewish people are still His people, then this gift is still theirs. And although it is only the means to an end, the physical territory of Israel is very much intertwined with its spiritual territory.

As it was in the past, so it is today. The ownership of the land was unconditional, although its occupancy was not. Israel was first and foremost to be God's showpiece of blessing or curse to other nations depending on its righteous or unrighteous living. Israel's exile to Babylon showed that He could expel His people from their land if necessary and bring them back whenever He chose to. So the first exile lasted seventy years and the second one thousand nine hundred years. Both times, He warned them beforehand, first through the prophets and later through Yeshua, when they rejected Him.[3]

In AD 70, the Romans destroyed Jerusalem and rebuilt it under the name of Aelia Capitolina. The land was deliberately renamed Palestinia after the Philistines, who were the archenemies of Israel. But although the Jews were expelled from their land, their land was never removed from their heart. Year after year, through centuries of wanderings, their Passover declaration remained "Next Year in Jerusalem."

Meanwhile, many successive civilizations came and went, as follows:

324	Part of the Byzantine Empire
614	Part of the Persian Empire
629	Ruled by the Unmayad Arabs

750	Ruled by the Abbasid Arabs
878	Ruled by Egypt
1099	Conquered by the Crusaders who massacred Muslims and Jews
1187	Kurdish rule with Saladin
1250	Egyptian Mamluks take over
1517	Ottoman Empire
1917	British rule following the conquest of Jerusalem by General Allenby
1947	U.N. votes for partition of the Land
1948	Foundation of the Jewish state (not including the Old City)
1967	Capture of the Old City during the Six-Day War

All throughout the second exile, a token Jewish presence was maintained in what had become a barren land. Following his visit in 1867, Mark Twain wrote, "Of all the lands there are for dismal scenery, I think Palestine must be the prince. The hills are barren . . . the valleys unsightly deserts. It is a hopeless, dreary, heartbroken land . . . Palestine sits in sackcloth and ashes . . . desolate and unlovely."[4] Despite this, the Jews began to return in the last quarter of the nineteenth century, fuelled by the persecution of the Russian pogroms. At the cost of their lives, they irrigated malaria-ridden swamps and turned them into the fertile land that is Israel now.

During that same time, anti-Semitism was on the rise in Europe. It prompted Theodor Herzl to call a World Zionist Congress in Basel Switzerland in 1897. A program was adopted for the establishment of a Jewish homeland in Palestine, which he believed that "in five years, certainly fifty" everyone would see.

Following General Allenby's liberation of Jerusalem from the Turks in 1917, the League of Nations gave Britain the mandate to govern Palestine. The Balfour Declaration of 1917 clearly stated that "His Majesty's government view with favor the establishment in Palestine of a national home for the Jewish people, and will use their best endeavors to facilitate the achievement of this objective." But unfortunately, incompatible promises were made to both Jews and Arabs. As a result, Jewish immigration was restricted both before and after World War 2. The situation eventually became so intractable that the British withdrew in 1947. It left the way wide open for the Jews to declare a sovereign state and for the surrounding Arab nations to declare war on it.

The day after David Ben Gurion read the Declaration of Independence, forty million Arabs, of whom one and a half million were armed, surrounded six hundred and fifty thousand Jews, who were mostly unarmed. Together Egypt, Transjordan, Iraq, Syria, and Lebanon attacked the new state of Israel. Some of the Arab leaders called on the Arab population to leave their homes temporarily until Israel was driven into the sea. When it miraculously survived, over eight hundred thousand innocent

Arabs fled in fear to the surrounding countries, which in turn expelled a similar number of Jews. The Jews were quickly assimilated into Israel, but by contrast, the Arabs tragically remained refugees in the neighboring nations. All of this led to the entangled Palestinian problem that we know today and to much ongoing suffering for many Palestinian men, women, and children.

This and the secularity of Israel, which is by no means whiter than white, cause many to question whether the rebirth of the state of Israel was an act of God. Those who do not appreciate His sovereign right to give the land to whom He chooses can only regard Israel as an accident of history without any spiritual significance.

Yet scripture tells us that Israel would make a physical return to the land before making a spiritual return to the Lord. Meanwhile, it would be a work in progress. Jeremiah 33:7–9 promises, "I will bring Judah and Israel back from captivity and will rebuild them as they were before. I will cleanse them from all the sin they have committed against me and will forgive all their sins of rebellion against me. Then this city will bring me renown, joy, praise and honor before all nations on earth that hear of all the good things I do for it; and they will be in awe and will tremble at the abundant prosperity and peace I provide for it." Ezekiel 36:24–26 adds, "For I will take you out of the nations; I will gather you from all the countries and bring you back into your own land. I will sprinkle clean water on you, and you will be clean; I will cleanse you from all your impurities and from all your idols. I will give you a new heart and put a new spirit in you; I will remove from you your heart of stone and give you a heart of flesh."

To these prophecies can be added Ezekiel's progressive vision of the valley of dry bones,[5] the promise that God would repay the years that the locusts have eaten,[6] the ongoing call to pray for Jerusalem,[7] and the challenge to give ourselves no rest until God establishes Jerusalem and makes her the praise of the earth.[8]

Despite the disagreements and perplexity surrounding the question of the land of Israel, scripture confirms that what is going on today is very much on track with God's purposes. On the basis of His Word, the Jewish people are not disqualified from being its legitimate occupants. In His grace and faithfulness, He has brought them back in keeping with His promises of four thousand years ago. He who rules the nations decides who would own the land, and in His sovereignty, He chose to give it to the Jews.

Paul put it this way in Acts 17:26, "From one man he made every nation of men, that they should inhabit the whole earth; and he determined the times set for them and the exact places where they should live."

This in no way sidesteps the issues of human rights on either side. It simply invites us to get the necessary perspective to understand the why's and how's of Israel today.

The restoration of Israel to its land is only part of a much bigger picture of God's dealing with the nations. When God "brings princes to naught and reduces the rulers of this world to nothing"[9] it affects the lives of individuals and raises issues of justice that may seem intractable. It compels us to acknowledge that His judgments are unsearchable and His paths beyond tracing out.[10] If God's hand of justice is on the nations, it will especially be on Israel. He will use its inner struggle with sin and its outer struggle with its enemies to refine it and bring it to its Messiah.

Our calling is to intercede for Israel from the heavenly perspective and cowork with the God who has chosen to restore Israel "for a second time."[11]

Then the time will finally come when, as prophesied in Isaiah 11:13, "Ephraim's jealousy will vanish and Judah's enemies will be cut off."

FOOTNOTE 5

Should We Repent?

HAVE YOU FELT GOD's grief over His body turning its back on Israel and the Jews? If you have, did you also wonder if it was possible to repent for the sin of past generations?

I thought long and hard about this knowing that no amount of repentance would actually change the story. As I prayed for clarity, God answered my question by first dealing with my own heart.

I had been a pastor for thirty years and thought that I had done a relatively good job of pastoral ministry. But the Lord convicted me that it had often been a case of getting it right for the wrong reasons. His grace had covered my weaknesses and inadequacies, but underneath my apparent confidence had been the unresolved wounding of childhood. My striving to compensate had been the driving force of my leadership, and it had fallen short of the love test of 1 Corinthians 13.

God also showed me how much the sins and traumas of my ancestors had shaped my identity and my reactions to the pressures of life. Although the buck stopped with me for the wrong choices I had made, I had been the victim of my family's dysfunctionality.

My genealogy was a case study of how children bear the sins of their forefathers to the fourth generation.[1] I had been born into a rolling emotional debt which was passed down from generation to generation.

I knew I could not change the past, but by the power of Yeshua's blood, I could be free from it. To complete my own reformation, I needed to halt the domino effect of my ancestors' sin. When I confessed my sins and theirs, God showed me how their ungodly beliefs and behaviors had bound my life. He delivered me from the generational burdens that affected my early development and then went on to rewire me as the person He intended me to be.

This personal breakthrough was a confirmation that confessing the sins of our ancestors was still very much on God's agenda. I discovered it was a pattern He had first established in Leviticus regarding the nation of Israel.

"If they will confess their sins and the sins of their fathers . . . then when their uncircumcised hearts are humbled and they pay for their sin, I will remember my covenant with Jacob and my covenant with Isaac and my covenant with Abraham, and I will remember the land."[2]

God required the Israelites to confess their fathers' sins insofar as they were known but did not require the Israelite's to repent on their fathers' behalf. In the same way, He does not require us to repent for the sins that others have committed. In fact, what is sometimes referred to as "identificational repentance" is an unreachable goal because true repentance has to be followed by corresponding actions.[3] But as Jeremiah, Daniel, Ezra, and Nehemiah understood, we do have to confess our ancestors' sins if we are to be free of their effects.

Jeremiah prayed passionately, "Let us lie down in our shame, and let our disgrace cover us. We have sinned against the Lord our God, both we and our fathers; from our youth till this day we have not obeyed the Lord our God."[4]

Daniel, foreseeing the desolation of Jerusalem, pleaded with God in sackcloth and ashes and confessed, "O Lord, the great and awesome God, who keeps His covenant of love with all who love Him and obey His commands, we have sinned and done wrong. We have been wicked and have rebelled; we have turned away from your commands and laws. We have not listened to your servants the prophets, who spoke in your name to our kings, our princes and our fathers, and to all the people of the land . . ."[5]

Ezra, appalled at the intermarriage of Israelites to pagan wives, fell on his knees and prayed, "O my God, I am too ashamed and disgraced to lift up my face to you, my God, because our sins are higher than our heads and our guilt has reached to the heavens. From the days of our forefathers until now, our guilt has been great . . ."[6]

Nehemiah, weeping over the dereliction of Jerusalem, cried out, "O Lord, God of heaven, the great and awesome God, who keeps His covenant of love with those who love Him and obey His commands, let your ear be attentive and your eyes be open to hear the prayer your servant is praying before you day and night for your servants, the people of Israel. I confess the sins we Israelites, including myself and my father's house, have committed against you. We have acted very wickedly towards you. We have not obeyed the commands, decrees and laws you gave your servant Moses . . ."[7]

These great men are our role models. None of them repented on behalf of their forefathers, but all of them prayed that His forgiveness would free their generation from the recurrent effects of ancestral sins. They humbled themselves before Him, believing that He would be merciful to forgive, to hear, and to act because they bore his name.[8]

We cannot change the history of the Church, but we can affect its future by acknowledging and confessing centuries of anti-Semitism and replacement theology.

Before that, we must first repent of our own sin of dishonoring God's purposes for Israel. This includes any indifference since "all it requires for evil to prevail is for good people to do nothing."[9]

Then, as He promised, God will create in us new patterns of thinking and behavior and increasingly make us the people He intended us to be.

NOTES

CHAPTER 1

1. John Knox quoted in John T. McNeil, *The History and Character of Calvinism.*
2. Church with a capital 'C' refers to the institutional Church, whilst church with a small 'c' refers to the body of believers as described in Ephesians 1:22–23 and Colossians 1:24.
3. Martin Luther, preface to *Commentary on Epistle of Paul the Apostle to the Romans.*
4. William Montner, *Calvin's Geneva.*
5. A. L. Herminjard, *Correspondence des Réformateurs dans les Pays de Langue Française, Volume 1.*
6. *Encyclopedia Judaica.*
7. Martin Luther, *That Jesus Christ Was Born a Jew.*
8. Ibid.
9. Martin Luther, *The Jews and Their Lies.*
10. J. Lange van Ravenswaay, *Calvin and the Jews.*
11. John Calvin, *Responses to Questions and Objections of a Certain Jew.*
12. John Calvin, *Commentary on the Epistle of the Apostle Paul to the Romans.*

13. John Calvin, *Commentary on the Epistle of the Apostle Paul to the Galatians.*
14. Jack Hughes Robinson, *John Calvin and the Jews.*
15. Martin Luther, *The Jews and Their Lies.*

CHAPTER 2

1. Alban Butler, *Lives of the Saints.*
2. Robert S. Wistrich, *Anti-Semitism.*
3. Ibid.
4. Ambrose, *Letter to Theodosius about the Affair of the Synagogue in Callinicum.*
5. *Encyclopedia Judaica.*
6. David H. Stern, *Messianic Judaism.*
7. Jeremiah 31:3.
8. Jeremiah 31:37.
9. Isaiah 43:1.
10. Exodus 19:5.
11. Genesis 17:7.
12. Romans 11:1.
13. Romans 11:29.
14. John 14:6.
15. Ephesians 2:8.
16. 1 Timothy 5:19.
17. Adolf Hitler, Speech April 12, 1922.
18. Isaiah 55:8.
19. Romans 11:33–35.
20. Romans 1:16.

21. Jeremiah 9:6.
22. Jeremiah 24:3.
23. Romans 11:17.

CHAPTER 3

1. Matthew 15:24.
2. Acts 17:2, 21:24, and 25:8.
3. Acts 15:6–29.
4. Alister E. McGrath, *Christianity: An Introduction*.
5. Luke 2:42.
6. Luke 4:16.
7. Genesis 22:18.
8. Isaiah 11:1–5.
9. Revelation 5:5.
10. Esther 3:13.
11. Jerusalem Post, *An Ominous Reckoning*, November 8, 2011.
12. Isaiah 14:13–14.
13. Deuteronomy 32:10.
14. Revelation 20:7.
15. Mark 13:22.
16. Matthew 24:12.
17. Romans 1:16.
18. Ephesians 3:10–11.
19. Ray Stedman, *The Manifold Wisdom of God's Love*.
20. Matthew 16:13.

CHAPTER 4

1. Luke 8:11.
2. John 1:1.
3. Hosea 10:11–12.
4. Romans 1:17.
5. Isaiah 49:6.
6. Genesis 12:2–3.
7. Genesis 11:1–9.
8. Exodus 19:5.
9. Deuteronomy 7:7.
10. Exodus 19:6.
11. Deuteronomy 32:10.
12. Jeremiah 31:3.
13. Jeremiah 31:32.
14. Jeremiah 31:35–37.
15. Genesis 17:7.
16. Genesis 32:22–28.
17. Jeremiah 2:13–15.
18. 1 Peter 5:8.
19. 1 Kings 19:18.
20. Jeremiah 29:11 and 14.
21. Romans 11:26.
22. Galatians 3:28.
23. Romans 11:29.
24. Ephesians 2:14–16.
25. Zechariah 12:10.
26. Zechariah 13:1.

27. Zechariah 13:9.
28. Zechariah 14:1–4.
29. Zechariah 14:8–9.
30. Zechariah 14:16.
31. Isaiah 55:10–11.

CHAPTER 5

1. Matthew 13:24.
2. Jeremiah 16:14.
3. Michael Elkins, *Forged in Fury.*
4. James 4:7.
5. Ephesians 6:11.
6. 2 Corinthians 2:11.
7. Matthew 12:30.
8. Psalm 139:23–24.
9. Romans 12:2.
10. Romans 11:18.
11. Zechariah 12:3.
12. Genesis 9:20–23.
13. Romans 11:33–35.
14. Genesis 12:1–3.
15. Luke 7:2–10.
16. John 4:22.
17. Romans 11:11.
18. Psalm 118:26.
19. Psalm 122:6.
20. 1 John 3:18.

21. Ephesians 2:12.
22. Romans 9:4.
23. Ephesians 2:13.
24. Galatians 3:29.
25. Of the 13 million Jews worldwide, almost half are now back in the land of Israel. However, of the estimated 250,000 Messianic believers worldwide, only some 10,000–15,000 are in the land of Israel.
26. Zechariah 14:8–9.

CHAPTER 6

1. Romans 11:26–27.
2. Romans 11:25 (compare the NIV with the KNJV).
3. 1 Corinthians 10:26 (KNJV).
4. Colossians 2:9.
5. Ephesians 1:23.
6. Romans 9:27.
7. Luke 21:24.
8. Romans 1:17.
9. Matthew 6:33.
10. John Calvin, *Institutes of the Christian Religion*, chapter XXV, section 5.
11. John Calvin, *Commentary Upon The Acts of The Apostles*, Acts 1:6.
12. Ibid., Acts 1:8.
13. Augustine, *The City of God,* book 20, chapter 7.
14. Martin Luther, *Preface to the September Testament.*

15. Matthew 11:12.
16. Revelation 4:9–11.
17. Revelation 5:6.
18. Genesis 49:8–10.
19. Isaiah 11:1 and 3–5.
20. Daniel 7:27.
21. Jude 1:14–15.
22. 1 Corinthians 6:2–3.
23. 1 Corinthians 13:12 (KJV).
24. Hosea 11:8 and 10–11.

FOOTNOTE 1

1. Jeremiah 31:31–34.
2. Deuteronomy 32:10.
3. Acts 21:20.
4. Acts 21:23–24 and 25:7–8.
5. Acts 22:3.
6. Acts 16:3.
7. Genesis 12:1–7, Jeremiah 31:35–37.
8. Romans 11:1–2.
9. Romans 11:29.
10. John 4:22.
11. Romans 11:17–23.
12. Jeremiah 31:31.
13. Romans 11:17.
14. Psalm 122:6, Isaiah 62:6–7.
15. Matthew 24:12.

FOOTNOTE 2

1. 2 Corinthians 1:20.
2. Hebrews 4:14.
3. Acts 1:15.

FOOTNOTE 3

1. Romans 6:14.
2. Matthew 5:17.
3. Romans 3:31.
4. For a fuller treatment, see David Pawson, *Defending Christian Zionism*.
5. Genesis 8:22.
6. Matthew 5:45.
7. Genesis 12:2–3.
8. Genesis 17:7.
9. Genesis 26:4.
10. Deuteronomy 5:2–3.
11. Jeremiah 31:31–32.
12. Hebrews 10:1.
13. Romans 10:4.

FOOTNOTE 4

1. Dr. Jacques Gauthier, *Sovereignty over the Old City of Jerusalem*.
2. Genesis 35:12.
3. Luke 19:44.

4. Mark Twain, *Innocents Abroad*.
5. Ezekiel 37:1–14.
6. Joel 2:25–27.
7. Psalm 122:6.
8. Isaiah 62:6–7.
9. Isaiah 40:23.
10. Romans 11:33–34.
11. Isaiah 11:11.

FOOTNOTE 5

1. Exodus 20:5.
2. Leviticus 26:40–42.
3. Matthew 3:8.
4. Jeremiah 3:25.
5. Daniel 9:4–6.
6. Ezra 9:6–7.
7. Nehemiah 1:4–7.
8. Daniel 9:17–18.
9. Edmund Burke.

ABOUT THE AUTHORS

Derek Frank's dramatic journey of unearthing the Great Deception started on a flight to Israel in 1980. He was praying that God would send his future wife to sit in the seat next to him, and was keenly anticipating what God might do. But instead of a beautiful young woman, a Jewish boy sat down next to him, and he spent the entire flight feeling bewildered, watching the boy play with a Rubik's Cube. Every so often the boy would take the whole thing apart and reassemble it in its original form. As Derek descended from the plane he felt the Lord say "Your first love must be for my people who struggle with a puzzle they cannot solve." This started Derek's quest for revelation, inspired over two decades by visions, words of knowledge and study as he gradually uncovered one of the greatest deceptions of all time – the conspiracy to cover up the Church's true relationship with Israel.

Derek and Françoise met in Jerusalem in the early 1980s, where Françoise had been working as a nurse. This started a partnership that would bring them through three decades of pastoral ministry, eventually leading them to launch Roaring Lion Productions – a multimedia company focused on teaching Gentiles and Jews about the Jewish roots of the Christian faith and the importance of Israel in God's plans.